Zen Radicals, Rebels, and Reformers

ZEN RADICALS, REBELS, AND REFORMERS

Perle Besserman and Manfred B. Steger

Wisdom Publications • Boston

Wisdom Publications
199 Elm Street
Somerville MA 02144 USA
www.wisdompubs.org

An earlier edition of this book was published under the title *Crazy Clouds*.

Library of Congress Cataloging-in-Publication Data
Besserman, Perle, 1938-
  Zen Radicals, Rebels, and Reformers / Perle Besserman and Manfred B. Steger.
    pages cm
  Includes bibliographical references and index.
  ISBN 0-86171-691-4 (pbk. : alk. paper)
  1. Zen priest—Biography. I. Steger, Manfred B., 1961– II. Title.
  BQ9298.B47 2011
  294.3'9270922—dc22
  [B]   2010043293

15 14 13 12 11
5   4   3 2 1

Cover design by Phil Pascuzzo. Interior design by Tony Lulek. Set in Bembo 12/17.

For the Princeton Area Zen Group

Contents

Acknowledgments

Thanks are due to the late Robert and Anne Aitken for providing personal recollections of Nakagawa Soen and Nyogen Senzaki, as well as books and other materials relating to their Zen experience in Japan and the United States. We are indebted to the scholars, translators, and historians listed in our bibliography, whose dedicated work with original sources made this book possible. The late Professor David Chappell of the Religion Department of the University of Hawaii was most helpful in rendering scholarly assistance on the topic of Zen Buddhism, particularly regarding the chapter on Hakuin. Our dear Dharma sister Jennie Peterson maintains a lively Zen dialogue that continues still. We also want to thank the following Dharma friends: Bill Boyle, Hetty Baiz, and the members of the Princeton Area Zen Group, Paul Boston, Jeff Shore, Uschi Baatz, and Rev. Thich Thong Hai.

To the late Robert Aitken Roshi we gassho in gratitude for his guidance in our Zen practice with the Diamond Sangha in Honolulu.

Finally, to the Zen radicals, rebels, and reformers in this book, and everywhere, we extend our hand.

The aim of life, its only aim, is to be free. Free of what? Free to do what? Only to be free, that is all. Free through ourselves, free to be sad, to be in pain; free to grow old and die. That is what our soul desires, and this freedom it must have; and shall have.

—*R.H. Blyth*

Introduction

The Zen story begins in India five centuries before Christ with the Buddha meditating under the bodhi tree and coming out of meditation to see the morning star. Realizing that his self-nature and that of all beings was one and the same, and, moreover, that it was completely empty, Buddha became a wandering teacher. For forty years, he proclaimed his message: all things are transient, all things are interdependent, and all things are empty. Nothing abides, not even an "*I*." There is no God or Ultimate Truth behind phenomena; everything just is.

Despite the Buddha's warnings, his insistence on the individual experience of these truths by means of meditation, and despite his advocacy of a "middle way" that shunned asceticism as much as it did hedonism, Buddha's practice became a widely doctrinal system, caught up in rituals and scholasticism. After his death, his disciples split up into sects, many advocating the very means and ends against which their teacher had warned.

In the first century of the Common Era, in an attempt to recapture the middle way, Buddhist philosopher Nagarjuna documented the Buddha's discoveries. Nagarjuna argued that the mind never attains real substance, either in itself or in outside objects, and he attempted to deliver Buddhists from dualistic notions of soul or divine self while negating idealists of the "mind-only" school. Basing his claim on the direct experience of realization, Nagarjuna depicted the world and the self as "empty," or "such as it is," free of all metaphysical speculation, or will and representation. The West has translated this as nihilism. Buddhists call it deliverance. In the dissolution of the ego they find the end of suffering, not the black hole of nothingness, but an infinite ocean of effulgence, one with the process of things as they are. This truth, said Nagarjuna, communicates itself to the mind in the living experience of enlightenment.

Five centuries later, the Central Asian reformer Bodhidharma took his message of meditation on a dangerous journey east-ward—creating Chinese Ch'an, or Zen Buddhism, in the process. Bodhidharma may be real or legendary, but the impor-tant thing is that his name bears the radical stamp of Buddhist practice, the unequivocal insistence on the individual experi-ence of "everything just as it is." His successors in China, Korea, Japan, and the West still use the same tool of meditation used by the Buddha under the bodhi tree to reveal the living fact of *shunyata*, or emptiness. Bodhidharma was not a philosopher, and Zen is not a philosophy, nor belief in an abstraction, nor faith in a religious construct. Bodhidharma was a practitioner of Zen meditation, a man who expressed the experiential fact of self-realization, in which the narrow identification with "person" drops away, leaving one's self as the birdsong, the sound of the wave dashing against the reef, or the coffee perking in the kitchen.

Realizing their teacher's message, Bodhidharma's followers saw that, indeed, there was nothing holy, that the sacred and profane were not opposed, and that the ordinary moment, the ordinary event was holy just as it was. Suddenly, picking a flower, eating a rice cake, or making love was as sacred as prostrating before the Buddha or chanting his name. Nevertheless, traditional Chinese

Buddhists held fast to the idea that the Buddha and the patriarchs, and even Bodhidharma himself, were special beings, even gods. Many Zen practitioners stopped meditating and started to pray to these "superhuman" beings to intercede for them and create a miracle. To counter this, Zen masters had to resort to radical means. Take Hsuan-chien, a ninth-century Chinese Zen teacher, who lectured from the pulpit:

> There are neither Buddhas nor Patriarchs; Bodhidharma was only an old bearded barbarian. Sakyamuni [Buddha] and [his successor] Kasyapa, [the Bodhisattvas] Manjusri and Samantabhadra, are only dungheap coolies.... Nirvana and bodhi are dead stumps to tie your donkeys. The twelve divisions of the sacred teachings are only lists of ghosts, sheets of paper fit only for wiping the pus from your boils.

The tendency of students, however, to revert to dependence on gods, the Buddha, and the "holy" scriptures persisted. We find the eighteenth-century Japanese Zen master Hakuin similarly rebuking a student with: "Nothing can shine in your asshole." Clearly, the danger of such pronouncements lies in the possibility that they will be imitated by teachers who have not experienced realization themselves. And indeed, this sort of iconoclasm did lead to antinomianism in Zen circles in the past, and to scandalous behavior among so-called Zen masters that still occurs today. This book is not concerned with scandal. It focuses on those religious Zen geniuses whose training, commitment, and realization experience led them to a free life, unconstrained by religious etiquette, rules, or hierarchy. Exploring the lives of these great nonconformists can perhaps help to clarify this grey area in

Zen, overturning misconceptions about its antic or ascetic extremes and returning to a middle way.

Crazy Cloud, the pen name assumed by Ikkyu—Zen poet, painter, calligrapher, and wandering teacher—is a pun on the Japanese word *unsui*, the Buddhist monk whose detachment from worldly life has him drifting like a cloud over water. The Crazy Clouds of this book are those innovative Zen radicals, rebels, and reformers, the wandering seekers and sages often disguised as beggars, nomadic preachers, tree dwellers, and sometimes even madmen, whose singular Zen Way has profoundly influenced traditional practices of meditation, daily life, spiritual, social, and political attitudes in Zen Buddhism even to the present. Set within the historical thematic framework of Zen Buddhist practice from its inception in China, and its attitudes toward meditation, enlightenment, the teacher-student relationship, celibacy, lay practice, women, nature, social convention, and political climate, the lives of these Zen masters both reflect and contrast with the various religious movements from which they sprang and from which they departed.

Spanning the generations from eighth-century China to twentieth-century America, this book explores the lives and teachings of Zen reformers and eccentrics like the wry Layman P'ang, the fierce Rinzai (Lin-chi*), the renegade Ikkyu, the iconoclastic Bassui, the revolutionary Bankei, the innovative Hakuin,

---

* Because Zen came to the West largely through its Japanese lineages, certain Chinese personal names of ancient teachers may be more familiar to readers in their Japanese form. For such names, the Japanese form has been used with the Wade-Giles Chinese version given in parentheses following the first mention of the name. In the case of figures for whom no Japanese version of the name is available, only the original Chinese form is given. In cases where the Chinese name of a Chinese person is more familiar, the Japanese name has been omitted.

the poetic Soen, and the footloose Nyogen Senzaki. Their interpretations of the most radical forms of Zen Buddhism frequently proved too enigmatic and avant-garde for their contemporaries, but remain invaluable guidelines for their spiritual descendants in today's Zen lineages regardless of school or nationality. Even more significant for the modern world, these archetypal Crazy Clouds will particularly appeal to the contemporary Zen student steeped in Western norms of individualism, political engagement, liberation theology, feminism, and the destructuralization of all hierarchy, whether religious or social. These revolutionary Zen men are apt models for our own revolutionary times.

As we approach the second decade of the twenty-first century, the word *democracy* is on everyone's lips. Too often, though, the word is taken as mere lip service, passive agreement in the face of apparently legitimate authority. The democratic freedom of the Crazy Clouds reminds us of the unequivocal moral authority of the individual, which, in the last instance, must transcend all formal structures and find its own sovereign expression. No mere reflexive outburst against authority, the attitude of the Zen radical, rebel, and reformer—rooted in the fundamental tenets of Buddhism and expressed in a life that embodies transience, interdependence, and *shunyata*—proves that every concept, even the most noble, must self-destruct.

Like the Buddha himself, who is said to be still practicing, this constant examination of one's life—before and after enlightenment—the refusal to sink back into static oblivion, or, as the Zen masters call it, "sitting on top of the one-hundred-foot pole," is what marks the Crazy Cloud. Questioning all structures, abandoning all notions of having reached nirvana, he or she must paradoxically encompass and surpass them. This creative questioning of authority—rare in religious, political, and social life—is universally proclaimed in the centuries-old Crazy Cloud dialogue with us. We are encouraged by the Crazy Clouds' commitment and hard training, and by the true realization of emptiness that prompted them to take their experience out into the world and live as compassionate bodhisattvas. Their lives prove again and again that Zen always refers the individual back to herself or himself, that it always respects the individual disposition, the individual experience.

But individualism brings responsibility. Seventeen centuries after Nagarjuna, the German philosopher Immanuel Kant also argued that the mind had no real substance, that the phenomenal world was transient, and that God was yet another concept. He extended the Buddhist findings by proposing that every single rational agent, however temporary, must decide what is right, and that ultimate moral responsibility resides in the individual rather than in hierarchical structures. Kant did not negate the structures, just as Zen does not deny the world of form. Like the Buddha, who compared his teachings to a raft—useful and necessary in crossing a river to the other shore, but burdensome once there— Kant, too, saw that institutional structures could take one only so far before becoming a burden. Both men warn us that teachings, hierarchy, and institutions should be treated not as ends in themselves, but as skillful means in the eventual achievement of spiritual freedom and moral autonomy.

The Crazy Clouds invite us to walk with them on the razor's edge of essential freedom and moral responsibility. We must be careful about aping their eccentricity, or taking license for "creative anarchy." Without the experience of their hard-won realization and training, which in every case included a religious institution and a teacher, the mere imitator embarks on a dangerous and potentially immoral enterprise. At the most intimate level, Crazy Cloud Zen illustrates that meditation is a living experience, neither limited to monasteries and temples, nor bounded by time and national borders. It effaces the dour and taciturn image that many people have taken for Zen, emphasizing instead the joy in discovering that "emptiness is form" and "form is emptiness," and it embodies a vision great enough to embrace the Whole.

We begin in eighth-century China with the Layman P'ang, whose Zen partnership with his equally enlightened daughter and his refusal to become a monk despite his celebrated confirmation by the two greatest Zen masters of the age makes him an appropriate model for our own times, when fifty percent of Zen practitioners are women. Shattering the monastic code of Indian Buddhism that made it difficult for women to practice, P'ang never gave up family life, and took his daughter as his traveling companion and foremost disciple.

Not long after, Rinzai, the great Chinese T'ang dynasty Zen rebel, shocked the religious and political establishment when he grabbed priests and officials by the lapels and hurled insults at even the most socially elevated personages in his efforts to goad them into enlightenment.

The fourteenth-century Japanese master Bassui similarly shocked the Zen hierarchy by moving into a tree house and refusing to teach, after obtaining confirmation of his enlightenment from one of the great Zen abbots of the day.

Not long after Bassui's death, the quintessential Crazy Cloud, Ikkyu, came into direct and dangerous conflict with worldly power. As the illegitimate son of the Japanese emperor Go-komatsu, he was in constant danger of assassination despite his monk's status. But that did not stop him from embarking on a public fast in nonviolent protest against the devastating economic and religious policies of the Ashikaga shogunate; nor did it inhibit his egalitarian wanderings among the bums, beggars, and prostitutes who formed his "street parish."

In the seventeenth century, Bankei, the Japanese populist preacher, tossed out a corrupted koan practice and single-handedly overturned the religious establishment by preaching to the masses out in the open fields. Refusing to speak to them in traditional Zen language, he urged his listeners to realize the unborn mind in the baying of the wolves and the smell of the earth under their feet.

Equally stubborn, and as much his own man, Hakuin not only installed himself as abbot of his home temple and bestowed his own Dharma name, but revived and codified the koan practice that is synonymous with Rinzai Zen to this very day. Like his predecessors, Hakuin too broke all the rules, taking lay women disciples and interceding with the Japanese feudal authorities on behalf of the peasants comprising the largest share of his constituency.

Nyogen Senzaki represents Japan's great break with tradition. Born during the Meiji period, which introduced the forbidden West to an isolated nation, his antimilitarism and rejection of religious hierarchy so alienated him from monastic authority that he chose to go into exile. In the American West, Senzaki planted the fertile seeds of his own radical brand of lay Zen practice.

It was Nakagawa Soen, our contemporary, who sprouted those seeds. Improvising a Zen informed by Shakespeare and Hakuin, Beethoven and Rinzai, this poetic Zen master left his indelible stamp on Western practice and set into play for us the free and creative example that characterizes the far-flung family of Crazy Clouds.

1

P'ang Yun: The Family Man of Zen

Perhaps of all the Crazy Clouds, the story of Layman P'ang best reflects contemporary Zen in the West. The only significant lay Zen teacher on record in China, he carried his message of ordinary-life Zen outside the monasteries throughout his wanderings across Central China, refusing offers to become the Dharma successor of the greatest Zen masters of the T'ang era. Instead, P'ang created a sangha of family and friends and fellow wanderers along the way. His life was set against a tumultuous period in T'ang history, spanning the years 740(?)–811, a time characterized by Confucian court rule, high culture and literacy, almost continuous internal rebellion, and crushing Chinese military losses to Central Asian invaders.

In 712, after the fall of the fervent Buddhist Empress Wu, the throne was taken by Hsuan-tsung, whose forty-four-year rule was to be the longest of the entire T'ang dynasty. Reversing his predecessor's Buddhist policy, Hsuan-tsung restored both Taoism and Confucianism to their former positions of influence. Though he did not actively persecute the Buddhists, politics led him to regulate the vast social and economic power of the clergy by defrocking thirty thousand monks and prohibiting the construction of new temples. Any repairs needed on old temples were subject to review by government officials, and small shrines were no longer permitted independent status but were incorporated by larger temples. Monasteries were limited in the amount of property they could acquire, and monks and nuns were prohibited from preaching throughout the countryside and from selling Buddhist books and images on city streets. By 747, all clerical certificates were granted by government order only, and monastic institutions were subject to heavy taxes.

Hsuan-tsung met his defeat as a result of the machinations of his favorite concubine, the stunning young Yang Kuei-fei. Forced by his own military advisors to have her beheaded as the court fled from pursuing barbarian armies, the emperor surrendered his power to his generals, thus paving the way for the An Lu-shan rebellion of 755. In 763, the Tibetans conquered the great western capital city of Ch'ang-an, and Hsien-tsung, the new emperor, turned to the northern barbarians for help. It was a time of rapidly shifting loyalties in civil government, religion, and national identity. For the ordinary layperson it meant heavy taxation, twenty days a year of service to the state, and a serpentine bureaucracy that ruled every aspect of one's daily life.

After the An Lu-shan rebellion of 755, the system cracked. A revived Buddhism, which had flourished with the help of the power elite, lost its philosophical and aristocratic cast, leaving behind only popular sects like Ch'an (Zen) for people in the countryside. No longer hampered by court splendor and metaphysical intricacy, the Buddhism of the new order emphasized the ordinary life of ordinary people and took a simpler, more humane approach to human affairs.

Most of Layman P'ang's Zen career was spent during the reign of Emperor Te-tsung (779–805), whose strong-arm tactics and bolstered palace army provoked rebellion throughout the empire. The situation was so volatile that all provincial governors were expected to combine civil administration with military rule. So stringent were the emperor's attempts at reducing the regional economic and political autonomy that had prevailed before the An Lu-shan rebellion that, in 781, the northeastern provinces responded by gathering to make war on the throne. But dissension among the rebels themselves kept Te-tsung in power, and he managed to regain bureaucratic control of the empire by enacting a system of successful financial reforms. Eventually, however, Te-tsung fell under the domination of the military court eunuchs whom he had empowered to maintain civil order. His brief successor, Shun-tsung, could not rule, and so was ousted and ultimately replaced by Hsien-tsung, the emperor who ruled during the last years of Layman P'ang's life—a time of reemerging local, small-scale social organization. With no Confucian-inspired restrictions issuing from the central government, regional merchants developed their own markets and trade burgeoned. The emphasis on agriculture gave way to commerce, and a new system of silver coinage replaced the old rice currency. Strings of cash now became the means of exchange, symbolizing the breakdown of entrenched hierarchical ranking that had preceded the An Lu-shan rebellion.

It was not uncommon for men like P'ang Yun, son of a provincial Confucian administrator, to grow disillusioned with the lightning-speed shifts in politics and the economy and just opt out of the system. The resulting dearth of local bureaucrats thus placed the daily administrative authority of provincial towns squarely in the hands of military officials like Yu Ti, the governor of Hu-chou and Su-chou, Zen friend and patron of Layman

P'ang. Yu Ti ruled with an iron fist. He conquered the rebellious Wu Shao-ch'eng, governor of a neighboring province, and, for his performance, received the protection of no less than Emperor Te-tsung himself. This quite remarkable man of Central Asian origins reversed his cruel and arbitrary persecution of local Buddhists when he was converted to the faith by Tsu-yu Ho-shang, one of the successors of Zen master Baso (Ma-tsu). Becoming as ardent a Zen practitioner as he had been a persecutor, Yu Ti befriended Layman P'ang, visiting with him daily and engaging in lively Dharma dialogues. When P'ang died, it was the governor who compiled the only remaining record of the great lay Zen man's career.

Consider the situation of the average Chinese layman of the time. Peasants were forced to become tenant laborers, working often as indentured property for landholders, who, with the increase in social mobility, had built vast estates, creating a new provincial elite out of what was once itself a poor, land-hungry caste. The south became the center of the salt trade, while Kiangsi, site of the monastery of Zen master Baso, was famous as China's greatest tea-producing region. Small market centers dominated the business of the day, helping to increase the spread of small-town urbanization, with most cities doubling as garrisons for the ubiquitous armed forces. Self-reliant, these small urban centers provided the average citizen with the necessities of life, work, barter, social intercourse, and religion. Taxes on merchants were especially heavy; no wonder that so many wealthy businessmen encouraged their sons to escape social discrimination by taking government examinations and rising to bureaucratic or scholarly status. In light of the tenuous situation endured by most ordinary people living during these transitional years, with a central government breaking down around them, a fragmented social structure, and a fractious army stationed everywhere, it is amazing that a gifted Zen layman like P'ang Yun did not seek refuge in a monastery.

P'ang Yun was born somewhere around the year 740 and died a week after a solar eclipse of 3 August 808, only a few years before Rinzai was born. The brilliant and lively Zen centers stemming from the lines of "Dharma grandfathers" Baso and Sekito (Shih-t'ou) and placed in the hands of Hyakujo (Pai-chang), Yakusan (Yueh-shan), Nansen (Nan-ch'uan), and equally luminous others were his training ground. P'ang's dedication to lay Zen placed him among a group of the Buddhist faithful called *chu-shih*, practitioners who rejected the formal life of the monastery and generally preferred to remain outside the Chinese religious establishment. But this did not stop seekers like Layman P'ang from studying with the various Zen masters of the day, remaining in monasteries for brief periods and then moving on to sharpen their realization.

Given the name P'ang Yun, Lofty Interior, the only son of a Confucian small-town bureaucrat in Hsiang-yang, the Layman and his family moved when his father was promoted to prefect of the city of Hung-yang. Nothing unusual marks the story of P'ang Yun's early years: he did all the appropriate Confucian things—marrying, setting up a business, and fathering a daughter and a son. It was only shortly after his marriage, though, that he began to exhibit what his neighbors surely regarded as excessive concern for spiritual matters, adding a little hermitage onto his house and retreating there to meditate in the company of his wife, son, and daughter. Here, he wrote poetry and philosophized.

"How difficult it is! How difficult it is! My studies are like drying the fibers of ten thousand pounds of flax by hanging them in the sun." To this, his wife responded, "Easy, easy, easy. It's like touching your feet to the ground when you get out of bed. I've found the teaching right in the tops of flowering plants."

P'ang's spiritually gifted daughter, Ling-chao, who was to accompany him as his Dharma companion throughout his life, remarked, "My study is neither difficult nor easy. When I am hungry, I eat. When I am tired, I rest." Scant reference is made to P'ang Yun's son, Keng-huo, who remained at home to care for Madam P'ang by hiring himself out as a farmer when, sometime between 785 and 790, his father donated their house for a temple, filled a boat with all its contents, dumped them into the River Shao, and, along with Ling-chao, took to the road. To support themselves on their pilgrimage, father and daughter fashioned bamboo utensils, which they sold in the local market towns.

In 786, P'ang Yun appeared at the Mount Nan-yueh monastery of Master Sekito and asked him: "Who is the man who doesn't accompany the ten thousand dharmas?" Sekito responded by putting his hand on P'ang's mouth, and the Layman was instantly enlightened. He remained with Sekito for a year, practicing Zen among the monks as a lay student. One day the master asked him, "How have you practiced Zen since coming here to this mountain?"

P'ang replied, "There's nothing I can say about my daily activities."

"It's precisely because I know that you can't use words that I ask you," said Sekito.

In response, P'ang produced a poem whose last two lines have become Zen watchwords.

My daily activities are not unusual,
I'm just naturally in harmony with them.
Grasping nothing, discarding nothing.
In every place there's no hindrance, no conflict.
My supernatural power and marvelous activity:
Drawing water and chopping wood.

Sekito offered to make him a monk then, but the Layman refused, saying, "I'll do what I like." His next stop was Kiangsi and the monastery of the great Baso.

Here, he encountered the master in his first interview, asking, "What kind of man is it that has no companion among the ten thousand things?" Baso said, "Swallow up all the water in the West River in one gulp, and I'll tell you." At this, P'ang experienced still deeper realization and decided to stay on for a while, again as a lay practitioner. After a year, Baso, too, offered him the black robe of a monk in exchange for his "pauper's white robe," and once again P'ang refused. Perfectly confident in his Zen understanding, he challenged Baso, saying, "A man of unobscured original nature asks you to please look upward."

Baso looked straight down.

P'ang said, "You alone play marvelously on the lute." Baso looked straight up.

P'ang made a low bow, and Baso returned to his room.

The Layman said, "Just now bungled it trying to be smart."

This playful dialogue exhibits the guest and host metaphor so prominent in Zen koans of the Baso school. In this case, each person assumes one of the roles and exchanges it again, flipping comfortably between emptiness and form in a drama that perfectly integrates them both.

In his travels, P'ang made friends with an itinerant seeker who had worked as a day laborer at Baso's monastery, where he'd been convinced to shave his head and become a monk. Tan-hsia T'ien-jan (better known by his Japanese name Tanka, and famous for burning a wooden Buddha image to keep from freezing on a winter night) was a lively poet and unorthodox monk who, though he spent much of his time wandering with P'ang and Ling-chao, eventually became one of Baso's Dharma heirs. The two good friends traveled from monastery to monastery, testing their Zen wit against all who would take them on, and, along with Ling-chao, engaged each other in informal Dharma combat on the road.

Meanwhile, back home, Madam P'ang continued to practice Zen in the company of her son. A charming example of her enlightened understanding appears in Yu Ti's *Recorded Sayings of Layman P'ang.* One day she brought a food offering to a local Buddhist temple and was asked by the priest for the purpose of the offering so that he might post her name and thus "transfer her merit" from herself to others. Madam P'ang took her comb, stuck it in the back of her hair, and announced, "Transference of merit is accomplished!"

Since biographical information about the P'ang family's Dharma and daily-life activities is limited, we can only assume that they did not split up and go their own ways, but rather that they were in contact and that they all maintained their practice in their preferred style—Madam P'ang and her son as farmers, and P'ang and his daughter as peddlers. P'ang and Ling-chao eventually settled down, making their home in a rock cave twenty miles south of Hsiang-yang. Here, they were visited daily by the prefect Yu Ti, the outspoken official and part-time Zen practitioner who compiled P'ang's deeds, poetry, and Dharma wisdom.

The local people must have thought the P'ang family odd indeed. They had given up the relatively comfortable bureaucrat's life for indenture and itinerancy, and so removed themselves from their social sphere and put themselves in danger of starving. Though Confucian in upbringing, they identified themselves as Buddhists, yet refused to become monks and nuns. Though he had achieved enlightened Zen master status and approval from no less than Sekito and Baso, P'ang gave no lectures and built up no circle of disciples. He did not carry the traditional jingling bell staff of the Buddhist pilgrim, but rather the straight plain bamboo stick of the ordinary traveler. He wore his white commoner's caftan—which he called "my seamless robe of Emptiness"—without any desire or ambition to exchange it for the black robe that would assure his Zen reputation. The Chinese had little respect for white clothing; to this day it is still emblematic of mourning or frugality.

The *Chodang chip*, a Korean history of Chinese Zen masters compiled in 952, describes the Layman as "Confucian in appearance, his mind sporting outside of objects, his feelings unrestrained, and his conduct fitting with the true purport." It goes on to characterize P'ang's life as "turbid" and his attainment as "mystery-learned," his behavior as "easy everywhere"—with Confucians as well as with Taoists, with military governors and children, with his fellow peddlers, and, equally, with the most illustrious of Zen masters. His friend and biographer Yu Ti characterizes him as a "householding bodhisattva," a Chinese incarnation of the Indian Buddhist lay teacher Vimalakirti.

After two years in the rock cave near his hometown of Hsiang-yang, the Layman decided it was time to die. Sitting down in zazen (sitting meditation), he instructed his daughter Ling-chao to go outside and come back to inform him when the sun had reached its zenith. At twelve, he would die. Ling-chao went out and came back almost immediately, saying, "It's already noon, and there's an eclipse of the sun. Come and look."

"Is that so?" said P'ang.

"Oh, yes."

The Layman rose from his seat and went to the window. At that moment, Ling-chao jumped into his vacant place, crossed her legs, and, instantly, died. When P'ang returned and saw what had happened, he said, "My daughter's way was always quick. Now she's gone ahead of me." He went out, gathered firewood, performed a cremation ceremony, and observed the traditional mourning period of seven days before dying himself in the company of Governor Yu Ti. Yu had come to ask how he was. P'ang put his head on his friend's knee, saying, "I beg you to just see all existent phenomena as empty and to beware of taking as real all that is nonexistent. Take care of yourself in this world of shadows and echoes." Then he peacefully passed away. Yu Ti performed the cremation rites and had word sent to Madam P'ang.

When the Layman's wife heard of both deaths, she exclaimed, "That stupid girl and ignorant old man have gone away without telling me. How unbearable!" Seeking out her son Keng-huo in the field where he was hoeing, she told him the news. P'ang's son put down his hoe and, sighing once, died on the spot. Madam P'ang took care of his cremation ceremonies, then bid farewell to her friends and wandered off to a hermitage. She was never heard from again. The end of the eccentric P'ang family was not much different from the way they had lived: deeply, simply, and without leaving a trace.

P'ang's verse commemorating his radical lifestyle, his counter-Confucian approach to Chinese custom—which demanded absolute conformity to station in family, temple, and community—simultaneously reflects his social testament and his Zen.

> I have a boy who has no bride,
> I have a girl who has no groom;
> a happy family circle,
> We speak about the Unborn.

Layman P'ang's Zen teaching is embodied in story and poem rather than in sermons. His spiritual experience is the stuff of koans. He is forever coming and going, now engaging the monks of Master Yakusan in a dialogue about snowflakes, now sporting with his friend Tanka; always in the spirit of living realization.

One day, when Tanka came to visit P'ang in his cave, the Layman didn't get up from his seat. Tanka raised his fly whisk, symbol of the Zen master's authority. P'ang raised his wooden hammer.

"Just this, or is there something else?" Tanka asked.

"Seeing you this time is not the same as seeing you before," said P'ang.

"Go and belittle my reputation as you please," said Tanka.

"A little while ago you were bested by my daughter," replied the Layman.

"If that's so, then you've shut me up," Tanka said.

"You're dumb because of your intrinsic nature, and now you afflict me with dumbness."

Tanka threw down his fly whisk and left.

"Master Tanka! Master Tanka!" P'ang called after him. Tanka did not look back.

"Now he's come down not only with dumbness, but with deafness too!" said the Layman.

In such playful interactions, P'ang and Tanka express their totally unencumbered style of coming and going in absolute stillness. Reversing roles on another day, it is P'ang who comes in and stands before Tanka with his hands folded on his chest. This time, Tanka pays no attention to him. P'ang leaves, then comes back, and Tanka still continues to ignore him. P'ang sits down. Suddenly Tanka stands up before him with his hands folded. After a minute or so, he just as suddenly walks back into his room.

"I come in, you go out!" cries the Layman. "We aren't getting anywhere."

"This old gent comes in and goes out, comes in and goes out—when will it end?" shouts Tanka from his room.

"You haven't got the slightest comparison," says P'ang.

"I've gotten this guy into such a state!" exclaims Tanka, returning from his room.

"What have you gotten?" asks P'ang.

Immediately, Tanka plucks the cap from P'ang's head and says, "You're just like an old monk!"

The Layman takes back his cap, puts it on Tanka's head, and says, "And you're just like a young layman."

"Yessir, yessir!" Tanka laughingly agrees.

"You still have the old-time spirit," says P'ang. And Tanka throws down the cap, saying, "It's very much like an official's cap."

"Yessir, yessir!" echoes the Layman.

"How can I forget the old-time spirit?" says Tanka.

P'ang snaps his fingers three times, saying, "Moving heaven, moving earth."

Encased in an apparently rollicking confrontation, this discourse with mime is concerned with nothing less than the great truths of Buddhism: transitoriness, oneness, and emptiness—manifest reality displayed in the radiantly trivial gesture of pulling off a friend's cap.

In another such meeting, this time with Zen master Fujaku (P'u-chi), P'ang asserts, "Sekito's doctrine…melted ice and broke tiles."

"That's obvious without your mentioning it," replies Fujaku.

P'ang throws down his bamboo basket and cries, "Who'd have thought it wasn't worth a single cash!"

Fujaku says sagely, "Though it isn't worth a single cash, how can one get along without it?"

To this P'ang shows his agreement by doing a dance and leaving.

As he heads out, Fujaku holds up the basket and recalls him by shouting, "Layman!"

P'ang turns to look, and this time Fujaku does a dance and leaves.

Delighted, P'ang claps his hands, crying, "Returning home, returning home!"

Here, the two Zen adepts celebrate coming home to their essential nature with the very shouts and gestures of life itself. P'ang's teaching was informal, exemplary in the truest sense; his life was entirely devoted to enacting the Zen drama. Wandering from hamlet to hamlet in search of a worthy foil, he spent his days improvising his spirituality. Free of monastic rules and hierarchical duties, he dared to challenge the best and brightest of his day. Nor did he neglect the marketplaces and country roads, engaging mendicant monks and cattle herders as well as scholars and gentlefolk. In the lecture forum of a town where professional orators delivered sermons and discourses on the Buddhist scriptures, he once stood listening to a talk on the Diamond Sutra.

When the speaker reached the line referring to "no self, no person," the Layman called out from the audience, "Lecture master, since there is no self and no person, who is he who's lecturing, who is he who's listening?"

The lecture master had no answer, and P'ang continued, "Though I'm just a commoner, I know a little about faith."

"What is your idea?" asked the lecture master.

P'ang replied with a short poem.

> There's no self and no person,
> How then kinfolk and stranger!
> I beg you, cease going from lecture to lecture;
> It's better to seek truth directly.
> The nature of Diamond Wisdom
> Excludes even a speck of dust.
> From "Thus have I heard," to "This I believe,"
> All's but an array of unreal names.

The lecture master could only sigh in response.

Once, while selling bamboo baskets, the Layman slipped and fell. When his daughter Ling-chao saw this, she ran to her father's side and threw herself down on the ground next to him.

"What are you doing?" cried P'ang.

"I saw Dad fall to the ground, so I'm helping," she replied.

"Luckily, no one was looking," said P'ang with a smile.

A Zen woman of achievement, Ling-chao was as much her father's Dharma friend as she was his daughter. Portraits of the two depict them as a pair of sharp-eyed, alert companions engaged in daily activities. Between 806 and 820, father and daughter traveled north, stopping to sell their wares en route to Hsiang-yang, their mode of life captured in the three hundred poems the Layman penned to describe his mendicant, impromptu, everyday Zen style. Here are a few samples.

> Well versed in the Buddha way, I go the non-Way.
> Without abandoning my ordinary man's affairs,
> The conditioned and name-and-form all are flowers
>   in the sky.
> Nameless and formless, I leave birth-and-death.

And:

> When the mind's as is, circumstances also are as is.
> There's no real and also no unreal.
> Giving no heed to existence
> And holding not to nonexistence,
> You're neither saint nor sage, just
> An ordinary man who has settled his affairs.
> Easy, so easy...

To a seeker of perfection, P'ang offers advice.

> The past is already past—
> Don't try to regain it.
> The present does not stay—
> Don't try to touch it from moment to moment.
> The future is not come—
> Don't think about it beforehand....
> Whatsoever comes to eye leave it be.
> There are no commandments to be kept,

There is no filth to be cleansed.
With empty mind really penetrated,
The dharmas have no life.
When you can be like this
You've completed the ultimate attainment.

Speaking directly to all the Dharma heirs in his lay lineage today, P'ang Yun says:

Food and clothes sustain body and life—
I advise you to learn being as is.
When it's time, I move my hermitage and go,
And there's nothing to be left behind.

2

Rinzai: The Spiritual Storm

The T'ang period in China (618–907) is called the
Golden Age of Zen. In its earliest phase it may also be
called the age of innovation in art, religion, diplomacy, and business. It was a period of unprecedented cosmopolitanism that,
among other things, saw the invention of the newspaper and the
civil service examination. The T'ang emperors created a center for
monks, students, merchants, and travelers, who gathered from as
far west as Greece, and included citizens of Arabia, India, Persia,
Syria, Turkey, Samarkand, and Bokhara. The early Han dynasty of
the second century C.E. had already seen the penetration of Buddhism from India, transforming Chinese cultural life and institutions, and in turn being transformed by Confucian pragmatism
and indigenous Taoist attitudes toward nature.

The dynamism of the period bore with it, too, the problems of
centralizing a state that had been reduced during the "age of dis-
union" (the years between 180 and 581) to factionalism and
regional domination by powerful aristocrats. The entire T'ang
period saw the imperial government struggle to retain executive
power throughout the realm by wresting it from great clans who
were engaged in perpetual rebellion. Brought to its knees by the
An Lu-shan rebellion of 755–763, the imperial government was

reduced to dispersing its power to regional military governors who maintained total autonomy over their prefectures. It was precisely this form of provincial government that allowed independent, antihierarchical Zen reformers like Rinzai (Lin-chi) to change the face of Buddhism in China during the late T'ang dynasty and throughout the world thereafter. The emperor Hsien-tsung was on the throne when Rinzai was born sometime between 810 and 815; and Hsien-tsung and his successors were too busy suppressing rebellions in the Lower Yangtze and Szechuan regions, and restoring at least a semblance of bureaucratic unity over all but a few fractious northeastern districts, to be bothered with the small affairs of the eccentric backwater Zen priests who were Rinzai's teachers.

In 820, powerful court eunuchs usurped the throne, murdered Hsien-tsung, and, for twenty years, succeeded in breaking down the centralized bureaucracy by manipulating a series of weak puppet emperors. In 840, Emperor Wu-tsung saw his dynasty in crisis, faced by fluctuating foreign affairs and beset by financial disaster and continuous internal rebellion. Egged on by a fanatic Taoist minister, the emperor decided to solve his problems by focusing on the Buddhists as the country's enemy—a good excuse for seizing the enormous wealth of the monasteries and creating a new source of revenue. The Buddhist persecution lasted for only two years; then Emperor Wu died of drinking too many Taoist elixirs purported to bestow immortality, and his successor Hsuan-tsung (r. 847–859) decreed amnesty for Buddhists and tried his luck at financial reform and the codification of laws. But rebellion in the Yangtze valley and in the economically powerful southern regions disrupted his plans. In the northwest province of Nan-chao, war dragged on from 858 to 866, the year Rinzai died. For the entire span of this obscure Zen monk's life, China was engaged in war, beset by troops loyal often to no one, murdering and pillaging their way back home from one front or another. By 880, the great western capital of Ch'ang-an itself was captured and the emperor driven from the palace. Political and economic chaos ruled, until the total collapse of the civil administration marked the end of the great T'ang era in 907.

Unlike its contemporary in Europe, the Carolingian empire, the T'ang was not feudal but aristocratic, with nine grades of nobility, all related to the imperial family. Its first and greatest monarch, T'ai-tsung, created the Chinese civil service, promoting a social caste system molded by Confucian doctrines that still pervades Asian society today. The house of Li, from which T'ai-tsung claimed his legitimacy, expanded its territory halfway across Asia, opening the country to foreign ideas and disseminating Chinese culture west, east, north, and south. Ch'ang-an was the capital of the empire, the greatest city in East Asia, with more than two million inhabitants. Its markets and harbors were stocked with goods from India, Java, Iran, and Japan. Foreigners came to study Buddhism, to seek wealth, or to freely practice religions like Nestorianism and Manicheanism. In this atmosphere, Buddhists flourished, and, in 868, invented printing. The world's first book was the Diamond Sutra. Poets like Li Po, Tu Fu, and Po Chu-yi, and painters like Yen Li-pen led movements in art whose sophistication rivals that of the European Renaissance, which did not take place until eight centuries later.

Buddhism was the single most dominant foreign influence on Chinese life from the second to the eleventh centuries. It brought Indian monasticism into direct conflict with Confucian social and worldly hierarchy and notions of secular morality. During the T'ang, the Buddhist monasteries grew rich and powerful, holding vast estates, doing business, keeping slaves, and administering agricultural production of precious commodities like rice and oil. Monastics became money lenders, teachers, and political and spiritual advisers to important military governors, their influence spreading throughout urban centers in the south and at the imperial court in Ch'ang-an itself. But the T'ang court was also under the continuous influence of Taoism and Confucianism, and the three religions often clashed. The fate of any of them frequently depended on the whims and preferences of individual emperors, so it is no surprise that the An Lu-shan rebellion, whose military commanders were strongly Buddhist, should have led indirectly to the Buddhist persecution of 845. Military men were particularly attracted to Zen, peasants to Pure Land; and popular Buddhism, with its adoration of relics, its religious festivals, pilgrimages, and shrines, appealed to everyone. By the mid-ninth century, though, Buddhism had declined as a force in the affairs of state and as an intellectual movement. This was partly caused by the corruption of the monasteries, and by the enforced imperial sale of certification and ordination for the clergy.

The Taoists often attacked Buddhism most harshly as a foreign import, and urged a return to native Chinese traditions. Yet both Buddhist and Taoist priests were regarded as potentially dangerous agents of rebellion, for they represented much of the local peasantry, the marginal and disaffected members of the population. When, under Wu-tsung, in 845, the Taoists succeeded in their mission to expunge the "foreign import," over forty-six thousand Buddhist monasteries and temples were laicized, and four hundred thousand clergy were defrocked and stripped of their religious exemptions, properties, and slaves. Other foreign religions were persecuted as well; Nestorians, Manicheans, and Zoroastrians were forced to leave the country, and a new attempt at centralization from the throne met with a reasonable amount of temporary success.

Buddhist rituals at court had only been admitted to maintain the illusion that the emperors were no different from famous Buddhist rulers of the past. The faith was therefore doctrinally stable but politically shaky. Since ritual and ceremony were never the strong points of meditation schools like Zen, monks like Rinzai could carry on without attracting negative attention from the imperial authorities. This was particularly true in the north, where Rinzai ultimately settled and taught—an area that placed great emphasis on meditation and pietism, while the south focused largely on scriptural exegesis.

The travel diary of the Japanese monk Ennin, which begins in 838 and ends after the persecution in 845, documents the daily affairs of Buddhist life most accurately. He describes three categories of Buddhist officers: archbishops, bishops, and monastery supervisors and stewards. To earn money for their temples, such high-level monks as these traveled about giving lectures to the public on popular sutras, often attracting as many as eighteen hundred people. The lectures at the monasteries took the form of question and answer periods that were often combative, with much aggressive shouting and challenging from both audiences and speakers. Afterward, participants spent several hours in ceremonial chanting and shrine worship.

From the time the Zen school surfaced at the end of the eighth century under Hui Neng, the famous Sixth Patriarch, it proved an aberration to traditional Buddhists like those described in Ennin's diary—which refers throughout to Zen monks as "uncouth and rough-hearted fellows." Liang Su, a famous mid-ninth-century Buddhist author, excoriates his Zen contemporaries.

> Nowadays, few men have the true faith. Those who travel the path of Ch'an go so far as to teach people that there is neither Buddha nor law, and that neither sin nor goodness has any significance. When they preach these doctrines to the average man, or men below the average, they are believed by all those who live their lives of worldly desires. Such ideas are accepted as great truths which sound so pleasing to the ear. And the people are attracted to them just as moths in the night are drawn to their burning death by the candlelight.... Such doctrines are as injurious and dangerous as the devil and the ancient heretics.

Entrenched philosophical schools of Mahayana Buddhism like T'ien-t'ai or Hua-yen had little to fear from the Zen heretics until the An Lu-shan rebellion shattered the entire political and religious system. A spiritual counterpart of the individualist generals who participated in this movement, Zen perpetuated the active nonconformism that characterized the age in which it erupted. Not at all speculative, it appealed to the practical-minded Chinese man of action. It emphasized spontaneity and naturalness, and it did not clash with Taoist attitudes toward nature. It also bore a healthy distaste for institutionalism, and, unlike the vast landholding monasteries of rival sects that were often considered parasitic by the laity, its monks worked to feed and clothe themselves. Completely independent of scripture and doctrine, Zen teaching destroyed all notions of subject and object and operated in the often giddy realm of play and paradox. Its exponents broke with Indian quietism, idol worship, and metaphysics, preaching the direct and practical approach to enlightenment for all in everyday language that could be easily understood by even the coarsest Chinese peasant listener. Thus, while courtly Buddhism went into decline, rough-and-tumble Zen flourished, surviving even the great persecution of 845.

Both Zen and Taoist monks used the technique of breath counting that is basic to meditation to this day; both emphasized negation rather than worship, and the experience of emptiness as the basis for their practice. Zen master Baso established the great lineage that bore figures like Nansen, Hyakujo, Obaku (Huang-po), and Joshu (Chao-chou)—whose insistence on the "ordinary" way to enlightenment was often expressed in the most strange and extraordinary ways.

The life of the Zen monk was simple, consisting of hard manual labor and community sharing of resources. One slept and meditated on the same mat, patched one's own robes, and grew one's own food. Moreover, one's teachers participated in the work and indulged in what appeared to outsiders like Liang Su to be wild and antic pranks, shouts, and blows. While their doctrinaire Buddhist counterparts were spending their time adoring images of the Buddha in countless temples and shrines, the Zen monks were reputed to be burning those images and advocating the destruction of the sutras. What their critics did not understand was that an entirely new form of Buddhism was being fashioned in ninth-century China, one that removed all its Indian coverings, though using its legends, figures, gods, and heavenly realms as metaphors, and had plunged into the experiential reality of enlightenment in an entirely new way.

An obscure monk named I-hsuan was making his way south to Chiang-nan somewhere around 835 to study with the famous Zen master Obaku. It was this journey that was to culminate in the movement we call Rinzai Zen today. The monk I-hsuan had lived a very ordinary life, even according to the traditional Zen master biography written by the lineage followers who knew him as Rinzai. The boy I-hsuan, born somewhere between 810 and 815 in Nan-hua, Ts'ao prefecture, was called by the family name Hsing. Growing up in the region now known as Yen-chou-fu in Shantung, just south of the Yellow River, he found his monk's calling early and was ordained at the age of twenty. Not unlike many bright young men of his time, I-hsuan took up the path of scholarship, particularly devoting himself to an in-depth study of the Buddhist scriptures. He spent five or six years immersed in the esoteric philosophy of the Hua-yen and Wei-shih schools of Mahayana Buddhism. Then, one day, he experienced revulsion toward his books as "only medicines for salvation and displays of opinion," and threw them all away. This story is characteristic of so many great Zen teachers in the making that one wonders whether or not it became a formula: the bright young man, spiritually inclined, turns early to the Buddhist priesthood, delves into the intellectual tradition, and, longing for the direct experience of buddhahood, turns away from learning toward the teaching beyond words and scriptures. No doubt the luxury and corruption of the Buddhist monastic establishment were in marked contrast to the already ensconced line of Zen established by the great Baso and passed on to Obaku, whose shouts and blows and disdain for all traditional forms of Buddhism appealed to disaffected young monks like I-hsuan.

Joining Obaku's assembly, the young novice attracted little attention and was in fact so shy that it took him almost three years before he could gather the courage to face the great master in a personal interview. According to *The Record of Rinzai*, written during the Sung dynasty almost three hundred years after his death, he was noticed by the head monk, probably Bokushu (Mu-chou Tao-ming, who was to become another of Obaku's gifted eccentric heirs), and was advised to seek an interview with the abbot. I-hsuan followed the head monk's advice and went into Obaku's quarters, asking, "What is the cardinal principle of the Buddhadharma?"—a stock-in-trade question of novice Zen monks. Obaku's answer was a blow. Puzzled, I-hsuan returned to the head monk and told him of his experience with the master. Bokushu urged him to go back and ask again. Eagerly, I-hsuan sought a second interview and asked the same question. Again, Obaku hit him. Again he returned to Bokushu and related what had happened. "Go back and ask again," was the head monk's advice. For a third time, the hapless young monk returned to Obaku's quarters and asked, "What is the cardinal principle of the Buddhadharma?" Again he received a blow for his trouble. This time he went back to Bokushu and confessed that he had no idea what was going on, but, sure that there was some fault in himself for upsetting Obaku and getting beaten, he had resolved to leave the monastery. Bokushu, keenly perceptive, secretly went to the master and told him of I-hsuan's plight, recommending that Obaku keep an eye on the talented young fellow. Then he went back to I-hsuan and told him to say goodbye to Obaku before leaving. I-hsuan dutifully followed Bokushu's advice and went to pay his respects to the master. During the meeting, Obaku made casual reference to Daigu (Ta-yu), a colleague living in a hermitage not far away, suggesting that I-hsuan might there find an answer to his question.

The ingenuous young monk made off for Daigu's hermitage right away and, as soon as he arrived, stated his dilemma. But the cranky old hermit reproved him, saying, "You didn't appreciate Obaku's grandmotherly kindness." With these words, I-hsuan achieved realization and shouted, "Ah...so there's not much to Obaku's Dharma at all!" Daigu answered him with a blow, which I-hsuan returned in kind.

"Whippersnapper!" cried Daigu, "I've nothing to do with you; you're Obaku's problem. Go back to him!"

I-hsuan returned to his home monastery and greeted Obaku with a slap.

"You lunatic, coming back here to pull the tiger's whiskers!" shouted the master, delighted at his student's enlightenment. I-hsuan responded with a loud shout, the *katsu!* that was to become his hallmark as a Zen teacher thereafter.

"Take this madman back to the monk's quarters," said Obaku, laughing.

This apparently mad exchange marked the real beginning of I-hsuan's Zen training. Remaining with Obaku and traveling back and forth between Chiang-nan and Daigu's hermitage in Hung-chou province, he honed his realization. The Buddhist persecution of 845 saw him sitting quietly at Daigu's hermitage, making occasional forays out to study with Obaku's Dharma brothers Isan (Kuei-shan) and Kyozan (Yang-shan), but always returning to his home base in Chiang-nan. The interchanges between I-hsuan and Obaku throughout these training years provide a living picture of two religious geniuses in action.

Once, at work, hoeing the ground, I-hsuan saw Obaku coming

and stopped to lean on his hoe. Approaching, Obaku called out, "Is this guy tired already?"

"How can I be tired when I haven't even picked up my hoe?" I-hsuan retorted.

Obaku hit him, and I-hsuan next seized the teacher's stick, poking him with it until the older man fell down. "Hey, fore-man," he cried out to the work leader, "Help me up!" That I-hsuan could knock Obaku down was in itself a feat, since the master was a seven-foot-tall powerhouse of a man.

The foreman came running and shouted, "Master, why do you let this madman get away with such disrespect?"

As soon as Obaku was upright, he hit the work leader.

I-hsuan went back to his hoeing, exclaiming, "They bury the dead all over. But here I bury people alive!"

This insistence on the absolute dignity of even the youngest man in the pecking order was not merely symbolic of Zen play-fulness, but a profoundly serious challenge to the imperial hier-archy of the T'ang code, where insubordination was a capital offense. Obaku's appreciation of such clear understanding of the "great matter" of life and death is illustrated by his consistent approval of I-hsuan's apparent rudeness. In a society riddled with Confucian notions of "place," these two freely improvised their spiritual drama of "revolution" and individual freedom.

Once when I-hsuan was asleep on his meditation cushion, Obaku came into the hall and hit the wooden sounding board with his stick. I-hsuan opened his eyes, saw who it was banging on the board, and went right back to sleep. Further down the hall, Bokushu, the head monk, was sitting diligently in meditation. Obaku hit the sounding board again and walked up directly behind him, shouting, "That young fellow sitting down there in the lesser seat is *really* meditating. You and your fancy notions—what do you think you're doing?"

Bokushu replied, "What does the old boy want from me?" Obaku hit the board once again and walked out.

Contrary to the teacher worship and miracle seeking that went on in the vast majority of Buddhist monasteries, these Zen students were exercising the finest display of the Buddhadharma. Perfectly "democratic" in their expression of insight, lucid and aware at all times of what they and their teachers were up to, they declared their basic human freedom in every gesture and shout. I-hsuan was consistent, behaving the same way even with venerable teachers like Tokusan. Once, while attending the old man, he responded to the master's assertion that he was tired by saying, "What is this old guy mumbling in his sleep?" When Tokusan hit him in response, I-hsuan pulled the teacher's seat out from under him. Tokusan got up and went back to his room. Most significant in understanding these apparently wild and unruly exchanges is that neither man is engaged in a contest to prove his superiority, that neither wins nor loses; the play's the thing.

Around 849, I-hsuan, now in his forties, set out on the traditional pilgrimage of the "finished" Zen monk. Mature enough in his understanding to challenge a host of famous teachers throughout the land, I-hsuan displayed his characteristic independence of spirit even at his parting from Obaku. As the master bid him goodbye at the gate, he offered him several articles he had inherited from *his* teacher, the great Hyakujo. "Here, take this armrest and lectern," said Obaku, symbolically granting Dharma transmission to his departing student.

"The Dharma has no need of such things," replied I-hsuan, "why don't you burn them?"

Obaku, who knew his Dharma heir intimately, said, "Take them along anyway. In the future, you'll cut off the tongue of every man in the world!"

Still, I-hsuan stubbornly refused, leaving without the armrest and lectern. Even at the last, an apparently ironic exchange signified the deep and abiding wordless connection between the two radical Zen men.

Having grown a beard and shoulder-length hair, I-hsuan wandered for over a year, testing his realization along the way with a series of famous and not-so-famous Zen teachers, always coming away with the confidence that none were any kind of match for him. Was this arrogance, or was it more perhaps an expression of the absolute freedom he had achieved? At last he made his way north, ending his pilgrimage in Chen-chou prefecture in Hopei. Here, under the generous patronage of the autonomous military governor Wang, on the banks of the river Hu-to, the monk I-hsuan became the teacher Rinzai, named after his temple Rinzaiji (Lin-chi Yuan), "the temple overlooking the ford."

Though Rinzai was left to his own devices by the local governor, he did not achieve great fame, and his temple always remained rather small and off the beaten track—no competition for the fabulous Wu-t'ai monastery atop the holy mountain that towered over Chen-chou and gathered thousands of Buddhist pilgrims from all over Asia. His popularity was modest as well; no record of a huge assembly of monks exists, though visitors appeared, both laypeople and monks; and even an illustrious Zen master like Joshu was known to turn up at his gate. But more important was the appearance of Fuke (P'u-hua), a mysterious divine fool of a man, the enigmatic helper who, it had been predicted years before, would manifest himself for Rinzai's benefit.

Fuke was an almost supernatural figure, appearing and disappearing from Rinzai's assembly, wandering through the marketplace, and goading even the Zen establishment with his riddles and pranks. Much of his style rubbed off on Rinzai, whose personal brand of eccentric individualism flourished in the short ten years of his teaching career. Their antic partnership is depicted in several vignettes appearing in *The Record of Rinzai*.

Rinzai and Fuke once went to a vegetarian banquet given in their honor by a local supporter. Rinzai presented a koan to Fuke while they were eating.

"A hair swallows the vast ocean, a mustard seed contains Mount Sumeru. Does this happen by means of supernatural powers, or is the whole body like this?" Fuke responded to the koan by kicking over the table.

"You ruffian!" cried Rinzai.

"What place is this to speak of rough and refined?" Fuke countered.

The next day they again went out together to a supporter's luncheon, and Rinzai opened the discussion, saying, "How does today's meal compare with yesterday's?" Fuke kicked over the table again, and Rinzai said, "You certainly understand it, but you're still a ruffian." This time Fuke replied, "You blind man; what are you doing preaching roughness and fineness in the Buddhadharma!" Rinzai countered by sticking out his tongue, an old Chinese expression of admiration.

On another occasion, Fuke, who came and went as he pleased, sometimes joining Rinzai's assembly, but mostly hanging around the marketplace, was sitting outside the meditation hall chomping on raw cabbage. Rinzai saw him and called out, "You have quite the air of an ass!" Fuke started to bray. Rinzai shouted, "This robber!" And Fuke took off, calling loudly, "Robber, robber!"

No mere exercise in one-upmanship, this kind of encounter served as a fine opportunity for sharpening Zen insight. No event was too ordinary, no place was unfit, and no person was too high or too low for Dharma play. Fuke, even more literally than Rinzai, was a homeless monk, but both were homeless in the truest sense, for both had abandoned all egoistic craving and notions of self-importance. And both were therefore at home everywhere.

Fuke, entirely outside the social order, a cartwheel-turning curmudgeon, used to roam about in the streets ringing a bell and crying out: "When it comes in brightness, I hit the brightness. When it comes in darkness, I hit the darkness. When it comes from all directions, I hit like a whirlwind, and when it comes out of the blue, I flail it."

Hearing this, Rinzai instructed one of his monks to grab Fuke and demand, "If it does not come in any of these ways, what then?"

The monk did as he was bid. But Fuke only wriggled out of his grasp and said, "Tomorrow there's a nice free lunch at the Monastery of Great Compassion."

When the monk returned and told Rinzai what had happened, Rinzai said, "I was always intrigued by that guy."

In perhaps the most folkloric of their exchanges, Fuke and Rinzai demonstrated nothing less than the central issue of Zen, the question of birth and death. Begging every passerby in the marketplace to give him a robe, Fuke refused all offers until Rinzai purchased a coffin for him, saying, "Here, I've had a robe made for you."

Fuke took up the coffin, slung it across his shoulders, and returned to the market, crying, "Rinzai had this robe made for me! I'm off to the east gate of the city to die!" People gathered and ran after the town fool to see what he was up to this time. Approaching the east gate, Fuke turned around and said, "No, not today. I'll go to the south gate tomorrow and die." This charade went on for three days, until the people stopped paying attention to him. On the fourth day, all alone, Fuke carried the coffin out beyond the city walls, got into it, and stretched himself out like a corpse.

A passerby obliged his request to nail down the lid and then entered the marketplace to report to the townsfolk about the strange occurrence. The local people all dashed to the spot, eager to see what Fuke was up to; but when they opened the coffin they found it empty. All that was left of the divine fool was the tinkle of his bell coming from high up in the sky.

Rinzai was reputed for his fierceness, Fuke for his antic disposition. Together, in the fashion of artists, they took Zen teaching into the streets and made it available to even the simplest shopkeeper. With no interest in propagating monastic Buddhism, without even a concern for the appropriateness of their podium or constituency, they lived, acted, and embodied the spirit of Hotei (Pu-tai), the bodhisattva of the marketplace.

The world around the small temple on the ford was in constant turmoil. Soldiers were everywhere, and invasions by northern barbarians were an almost daily concern. Politically, nothing could be more dangerous than preaching any sort of individualism or advocating abolition of rank. Yet it was here that Rinzai's unmitigated nondualism, his insistence on complete abandonment of religious dogma or dependence on external events, grew into the school that came to be known in Japan as Rinzai Zen. His immediate disciples numbered no more than twenty-five, with Sansho Enen (San-sheng Hui-jan) listed as his direct heir after the master's famous unorthodox last words of transmission:"Who would have thought I would pass on my Dharma to such a blind donkey!" It was only in the seventh generation of Rinzai's successors, with Sekiso Soen (Shih-shuang Ch'u-yuan, 986–1039), that his line spread south and overcame all other Zen schools of the Sung dynasty. The records conflict on the date of his death, one claiming that he died on 18 February 867, and another saying 27 May 866. Both accounts agree, however, that he was not ill, and that he seated himself and spoke to his disciples with characteristic humor and alacrity before closing his eyes and dying peacefully.

All the written information that remains of Rinzai's life and teaching is contained within *The Record of Rinzai* in the form of his discourses to students and visitors at Rinzaiji, and an appended biography. Though it was not collected for more than three hundred years after his death, it is nonetheless a vividly powerful testimony to the revolutionary, colloquial, even vulgar strength of Rinzai's teaching style. Indeed, he comes forth as a brilliant improviser, exhorting his listeners in shocking words and gestures always to be themselves. Using the direct Socratic dialogue approach, he invited questioners to challenge him in nose-to-nose confrontation, and did not hesitate to verbally and physically browbeat less than worthy opponents. Belying Rinzai's harsh exterior, though, is his remarkable humanism, his insistence on the unconditioned value of individual human dignity, a theme that was unheard of in the spiritual and social milieu in which he taught—in Taoism, which was nature-centered, or in Confucianism, which was preoccupied with social form and denied any autonomy to the individual, or in Buddhism, which was devotional and otherworldly.

For Rinzai, the human being was no philosophical abstraction, but a buddha in the flesh. His listeners were often as not shocked at hearing themselves referred to as bodhisattvas, buddhas, and patriarchs, and his patrons were probably no less abashed by his total disregard for caste or authority, expounded in his doctrine of the "true man of no rank."

One time, facing his audience, Rinzai cried out, "On your lump of red flesh is a true man of no rank who is always coming in and going out of each of your faces. Those who haven't yet verified him, look, look!"

A monk approached him and asked, "What about the true man without rank?"

Rinzai stepped down from his teaching seat and, putting his face close up to the monk's, said, "What about the true man of no rank?" Then, seizing the monk by the lapels of his robe, he shouted, "Speak! Speak!"

The monk hesitated, and Rinzai shoved him aside, crying, "The man without rank, how full of shit he is!" And he stalked out of the hall.

Rinzai did not teach anything new in Zen, but he radically altered the delivery of the message. He excoriated people for running back and forth between teachers, looking for enlightenment in the words and reputations of others.

I speak this way only because you seekers keep running around everywhere looking for the worthless contrivances of people who are long dead and gone. From my point of view, the Bodhisattvas are nothing but shit in the toilet, hitching posts for asses, prisoners in shackles. Buddha is merely a name!

Such demands for spiritual self-confidence were not for the timid or the devotionally inclined. In order to give living meaning to his words, Rinzai did not hesitate to shake, hit, and shout at his students, using "shock therapy" to enlighten them. Not surprisingly, he debunked quietism, and preferred action, live interchange, and gesture to long periods of meditation. He characterized sanctimonious monks as "a bunch of blind baldies who stuff themselves with food and sit like lumps for hours in meditation, stopping the flow of thoughts," and he warned them that sitting like this could only result in making "hell karma" for themselves.

Rinzai traded on radical statements like these, even going so far as to urge students to slay buddhas, ancestral teachers, and their own parents as well. Not surprisingly, these exhortations stirred up the opposition of Confucians, who were outraged at such disregard for filial piety. Traditional Buddhists, moreover, shrank from Rinzai's incitements to commit such "heinous crimes."

If you wanted to be Rinzai's student, nothing less than complete homelessness would do—not by becoming a monk, but by rejecting any sort of clinging to the phenomenal world at all. And this included meditation and the notion of enlightenment itself. For Rinzai, no "buddhas" existed. No past, present, or future could obstruct or bring about the experience of enlightenment. *Satori* itself required no practice. All that was left to the sincere seeker was faith in his or her own activity "right now." To all who continued questioning him about Buddha, Buddhism, enlightenment, and the rest, he replied, "The Buddha is you, listening to my discourse right now before my very eyes!"

Impatient with too much sitting meditation and with instructive techniques for prompting *kensho*, Rinzai often became frustrated at having to speak at all. Several lectures are therefore devoted to admonishing students for running every which way, looking around, scrounging Zen experience from "the secondhand words of others." For Rinzai, nothing but unconditional mental detachment *and* passionate engagement in the very activity of living itself would do. A tall order for a struggling young novice, no doubt. It must have been difficult to accept the master's rejection of traditional Zen instruction, difficult to abandon the cause and effect notion implicit in zazen that sitting would lead to enlightenment. Rinzai's insistence on immediate experience over induced tranquillity is beautifully illustrated by the following exchange with a rather self-confident monk.

Standing before the assembly, Rinzai said, "I spent twenty years with Obaku. When three times I asked him about the cardinal principle of Buddhism, he gave me three blows with his stick. It was like being patted with a branch of mugwort. I'd love another taste of that stick now. Who can give it to me?"

A monk stepped forward, saying, "I can."

Rinzai held out his stick. The monk tried taking it; as he did so, Rinzai hit him with it.

Everything in the Rinzai style of Zen lay in performance, direct speech and response, a dramatically perfect presentation of the whole. All the esoteric principles of Mahayana philosophy were condensed in a blow, translated into the challenging words of a dare. Today, Rinzai might be called a method actor, whose words and exaggerated, even distorted, earthy delivery convey nothing less than the profoundest spiritual experience. His genius tailored that experience for every individual confronting him. In interviews, he could "discern a man through and through" with his different brand of Zen insight, his refusal to make comparisons between secular and sacred. When detecting even a flicker of doubt in the student, a moment's hesitation, he'd let loose a blow or a shout to bring the student back to his center of confidence, saying, "One thought of doubt in your mind is the devil." Fearless in the face of ostracism from the Zen community, he advocated that his monks avoid hierarchy, temple security, and patronage, and warned them not to become temple masters who, like new brides, were terrified of being "thrown out with nothing on their backs." The really great Zen men, Rinzai said, had been outcasts from the start, and were recognized for their worth only years later. And that was, in his eyes, "a good thing, because if they were accepted all around, what would they have been good for anyway?"

Rinzai urged his listeners to avoid the "luxuries" of monastic life as much as he urged them to stop seeking for the Buddha. He encouraged them to be brave even in the face of miracles and demons. Nothing, not even gods, was permanent. How much less permanent, then, were the words of even the most venerable Zen master? "If you base your understanding on secondhand notes from some dead old guy," he scolded, "wrap up your notebooks in squares of cloth and declare them secret, you are nothing but a blind idiot. What kind of juice can you find in such dried-up old bones?" He preferred live discourse, the pungent dialogue, the dialectical paradox, and the apparently illogical twist. Take for example his discussion of Mind.

Mind is without form and pervades the ten directions: in the eye it is called seeing, in the ear it is called hearing, in the nose it smells odors, in the mouth it holds conversation, in the hand it grasps and seizes, in the feet it runs and carries.

Fundamentally, it is one pure radiance; divided, it becomes the six harmoniously united spheres of sense. Since the mind is nonexistent, wherever you are, you are emancipated.

Like the typical Chinese intellectual of his time, Rinzai was given to categorizing. Yet, the Zen man Rinzai used words and categories to shatter conceptual thinking, tossing lightning bolts to awaken the intuitive mind. He was very much a tutor, privately working the teacher-disciple relationship itself into a viable means for enlightenment. His own rich mind and psychological perception interacted instantaneously on multiple levels, so he had no patience for the slow and steady approaches of other teachers. He was therefore openly critical not only of Buddhist sects outside of his own, but of fellow Zen teachers as well, for not letting students "experience truth for themselves." A superficial reading of his techniques, the freewheeling blows and deafening shouts, might therefore obscure Rinzai's sophisticated doctrine of the fourfold relationship between questioner and respondent, whose process-oriented approach uses the guest and host metaphor to describe the transformation of the ego at work.

In the first situation, "guest," the limited ego, meets "host," the universal, or essential nature. Limited guest asks a question and is replied to by universal host. This is exemplified in Rinzai's own meeting with Obaku, when, in his unenlightened state, the young monk asked his three questions and got his three blows, delivered by the unencumbered and spontaneous functioning of the universal self.

In the second situation, "host" sees "guest"; that happens when the questioner takes the universal position and the respondent is the distinct ego. This happens when the enlightened Rinzai asks a question of his unenlightened student, or when an enlightened student answers from the point of view of his limited ego, the monk playing dumb, for example. Or, when the monk really responds from the level of dualistic mind.

In the third situation, when "host sees host," the questioner and respondent are both functioning as universal self. That is the best condition of the four. In this case, Rinzai's enlightened exchange with Daigu—striking the old teacher and saying nothing in response to his question, "What have you seen?"—is indicative of "host" greeting "host."

When, in the fourth situation, "guest" meets "guest," we are unfortunately in the condition where limited ego and limited ego meet in ignorance and misguidedly try to communicate. That, says Rinzai, is what happens during most student-teacher encounters: "There are some students who carry around their ball and chain and appear before a Zen teacher who just adds another lock to the burden. Student and teacher are very pleased, since both are unaware of what is going on."

In his "four processes of liberation from subjectivity and objectivity," Rinzai presents a koan, a blow, or a shout in order to free the student on the spot from the subject-object split mind. First, he takes away the person but not his objective situation, that is, he frees him from his attachments to the subjective world, but lets the objective world remain. To this end he uses poems totally descriptive of the natural landscape with no first-person perspective. Second, to remove the objective situation and leave the person, he eliminates all notions of seeking enlightenment from outside: "There are some Buddhist learners who've already made the mistake of seeking for [the bodhisattva] Manjushri at Mount Wu-t'ai. There is no Manjushri at Wu-t'ai. Do you want to know

Manjushri? He is at this moment working within you, unshakably, with no room for doubt. This is the living Manjushri."

Thus, liberating a student from both objective and subjective attachment is accomplished by a shout, a slap, or a push. Such physical shocks jolt the mind out of intellectual reasoning and free the person from identifying with either subject or object. This is dramatically illustrated in Case 32 of *The Blue Cliff Record*, a collection of koans still used in Zen centers today.

Jojoza (Ting Shang-tso) asked Rinzai, "What is the essence of Buddhism?" Rinzai descended from his seat, grasped Jojoza by the lapels of his robe, shook him, slapped him, and pushed him away. Jojoza just stood there.

"Jojoza, why don't you bow?" asked a monk in the assembly. As Jojoza bowed, he suddenly had great *satori*.

Finally, Rinzai lets both subjectivity and objectivity be as they are, perfectly identical with each other in a state of ordinariness, his ultimate reality of "Just shitting, pissing, and becoming ordinary."

By rejecting meditation and experimenting with new teaching forms, Rinzai even called into question traditional definitions of enlightenment and transmission. Yet he managed to implement a school of Zen that, though eccentric, was self-sufficient enough to outlast many of its hierarchical, establishment-based opponents. Alongside its friendly contemporary, the Soto line stemming from Master Tozan Ryokai (Tung-shan Liang-chien), Rinzai Zen developed unhampered by politics or religious institutionalism. Over time, however, its original creative power, the wild energy and freshness of its founder, was itself swallowed up by sectarian imitators and, in Japan, by the military, which ossified its spontaneous shouts and gestures into a "system." Rinzai's exchange with the military governor Wang, his own patron and student, thus rings ironically across the centuries.

One day, Governor Wang visited the temple and met Rinzai in front of the monks' hall.

"Do the monks here read sutras?" he asked.

"No, they don't," replied Rinzai.

"Do they learn meditation, then?"

"No, they don't learn meditation."

"If they don't read sutras or learn meditation, what on earth are they doing here?" asked the governor.

"All I do is make them become buddhas and bodhisattvas," Rinzai replied with a smile.

3

Bassui: The Lover of Sounds

Though he heard nothing but the battle cries of civil war throughout his life, Bassui found his great enlightenment in the sounds of the world. Born in Japan during the height of the Minamoto military dictatorship that spanned two centuries (1338–1500), Bassui's Zen developed against a political contest between rival courts and feudal chaos. In 1333, when Bassui was seven years old, the shogunate was overthrown in a factional attempt to restore the dethroned emperor. This spasmodic rebellion was unsuccessful and resulted in an open scramble between the shogunate and the imperial forces for control of the nation. Dislodged from their seat of power and culture, courtiers, poets, artists, and warriors became wandering Buddhists, emblematic of the deep sense of impermanence that characterized the age. It was a period of aesthetic melancholy that upheld the beauties of imperfection and sought refuge in the very instability that gave it life.

Living between 1327 and 1387, Bassui did survive to see a brief period of order under the shogun Yoshimitsu (1358–1408), and a patronage of the arts and Zen that overlapped into the world of diplomacy and trade. But the greater part of his own Zen career was spent in avoiding the slippery politics and the Zen hierarchy that fueled the "spiritual life" of the Muromachi era.

For more than sixty years, Japan was engaged in a struggle among feudal barons greedy for personal gain and eager to spread their names across the land. Even the great medieval code of knightly chivalry was wantonly abandoned in the open thrust for power. Obligation to lord and vassals narrowed to encompass little more than the immediate family or clan. The once great lords had lost control over their fiefs, and anarchy ruled. All sorts of adventurers, petty samurai, provincials, and stewards now rushed for the prize of land that had been wrested from the conquered imperial court. Rewards and punishments no longer rested in the hands of overlords; no feudal justice system of any kind presided. The intricate chain of power known as *shiki*, consisting of overlords, stewards, and provincial officers, dissolved, resulting in a crazy-quilt pattern of baronates with only nominal allegiance to the ruling Ashikaga shogunate. The division into southern and northern kingdoms that kept war alive provided a perfect backdrop for the shifting loyalties and legitimized banditry that were the order of the day. Kyoto was the constant scene of attack: first secured by the warriors of the southern faction, then retaken by the Ashikaga, then the Yoshiakira clan, and on and on, until the Ashikaga finally bought peace by offering the rival Yoshiakiras autonomy over six provinces.

In 1390, the Yamana clan, who controlled a sixth of the country, launched an attack on the Ashikaga. Again the business-minded Ashikaga bought peace, this time ending a war that had lasted for over thirty years by feeding still more territory to the insatiable Yamanas. In this fashion, the Ashikaga shogunate restored a shadow of order to Kyoto, at the same time creating a link with the outlying provinces. Samurai rule prevailed, which meant that brutality and corruption served as law and order.

Kyoto was filled with threadbare soldiers, fortune seekers, hedonists, and hucksters. The emperor was permitted to remain at court, ruling in name only, while the great military clans reveled in their mansions. One gang of samurai retainers even proved their brazen contempt for imperial power by brawling with palace guards and lopping off the branches of the emperor's sacred maple trees.

During Bassui's lifetime, the Ashikaga cultivated the arts more successfully than they managed their unruly subjects. This new, boorish military "aristocracy" sought respectability in imitation of Sung Chinese aesthetics and in Zen. To be modern meant to be conversant with all things Chinese; indeed, trade with China had proven to be not only an economic necessity but a spiritual one. Zen priests were imported along with rice, silk, and the arts. Under the Ashikaga shogunate, in fact, Zen Buddhism provided Japan with a whole new class of ecclesiastical businessmen who handled customs and duties as well as souls. Money changing was another lucrative priestly business. So powerful was the connection between religious hierarchy and trade that the merchant vessels sailing between Japan and the Chinese mainland were named after the great Kyoto temples.

The fourteenth century also saw the development of Japanese trade guilds, which survived almost entirely on the patronage and bribery of powerful monastery abbots. A fortunately placed businessman or skilled laborer could attach himself to a temple and be assured that the tax collector would look the other way. As always, the peasants were hardest struck; victims of outrageous transportation tolls and extortionist middlemen, they often resorted to violence against their secular creditors, but were virtually helpless against the power of their monastic overlords.

Consequently, in addition to feudal warfare, numerous agrarian uprisings accompanied the radical economic swings of the Muromachi period. Similarly, the individual family unit underwent a dramatic change, with all hereditary privileges reserved for eldest sons (who could presumably fight for the family land if necessary) and women now subordinated to the position of chattel. In situations where there were no sons to retain the family name, perfect strangers were adopted and given all due rights and privileges—a procedure that is still practiced in Japan today. The population was therefore entirely preoccupied with maintaining family prestige, securing a name and a piece of land. Even peasant and craftsmen's families were tracked by masters who sought the "right" to their services for posterity.

Within this rigid feudal way of life, patience and shame became virtues; guarding the family name and conforming to authority were elevated to the status of national social norms. For many luckless younger sons and daughters the religious life was the only refuge, as it was for a variety of spiritual seekers, malcontents, and independent thinkers. Monasteries were a safe harbor, too, for artists and poets who basked in the patronage of great Zen priests like Muso Kokushi (1275–1351). So powerful was this National Teacher of the shogun Takauji that he convinced the dictator to build temples throughout the land in restitution for the lives lost during the civil wars. Zen temple building rose to fever pitch, with Tenryuji, the head Kyoto branch, erected in only three months! Muso's memorable praise for Takauji, his primary Zen pupil, was that even after a night of heavy drinking, the shogun managed to put in long hours of zazen before falling asleep.

Such was the state of Zen when Bassui Tokusho was born to an obscure samurai family in the province of Sagami, Kanagawa prefecture, on 6 November 1327. While pregnant, his superstitious mother had dreamed that she was about to give birth to a demon, and so she abandoned the newborn baby in a field not far from her home. A family servant found the infant and raised it as his own. When Bassui was four, his stepfather died, leaving the child with a terrible fear of falling into hell. At a memorial service for his stepfather held when the boy was seven, a priest making food offerings at the altar was startled when the child asked him who was going to eat the food. "The soul of your father," he answered. "What is this thing called a soul?" the boy pressed on. But he could be given no satisfactory answer. By the time Bassui turned nine he was having nightmares about eternal damnation, waking up in the darkness and seeing flashes of hellfire in his room.

Growing up as a social outsider haunted by the agonies of the "three evil paths" of hell, hungry ghosts, and animals, Bassui began meditating early on life after death. Gradually, he refined his question, changing it from "What is the nature of the soul that can enjoy food and suffer pain after physical death?" to "Who is the one seeing, hearing, and understanding in this very moment?" As an adolescent he discovered that nothing could be called a soul, that all was in fact empty, and he was temporarily appeased. But one day he happened on a book and read, "The mind is host, the body is guest," and he was once again plunged into doubt. If the mind was host it couldn't be empty, he reasoned. Indeed, mind must be that which sees and hears, and understands that it does. But ruminating like this was getting him nowhere, so at twenty he went off to ponder his spontaneous koan under the guidance of Zen master Oe at Jifukuji, a temple in his home province of Sagami.

From the very start, Bassui refused to shave his head or practice any religious ritual. Dressed as a layman, never reciting sutras, he spent every waking moment in zazen, determined to discover "who was master." Coming and going from his home temple on pilgrimages, Bassui sought out the Zen teachers of the day, testing his question, but always refusing to remain with them as a monk, finding it more helpful to sit zazen in isolated mountain huts and even in trees. Once, hearing of a hermit monk named Tokukei Jisha, Bassui, his head now shaved as a concession to temple etiquette, but still dressed in layman's clothing, decided to pay him a visit. Looking out from his hut, the hermit called, "Why aren't you wearing monk's robes?"

"I became a monk to understand the great matter of life and death, not to wear Buddhist robes!" Bassui called back.

"I see. Then are you looking into the koans of the old teachers?"

"Of course not. How can I appreciate the words of others when I don't even know my own mind?" Bassui replied.

"Well, how then do you approach your religious practice?"

"I became a monk in order to clarify the source of the great Buddhadharma. After I attain enlightenment I want to save all beings, bright and dull, teaching everyone according to his or her ability. What I want most is to relieve people of their suffering even if I myself may have to fall into hell."

Tokukei was impressed and welcomed in the young unorthodox-looking monk.

Now in his twenties, Bassui engaged in meditation for almost a decade, until one morning, after having sat zazen the night through, he got up to wash in a nearby mountain stream. Suddenly the sound of the gurgling water gushed through him and he had a moment of realization. Having vowed never to announce himself without the confirmation of a real Zen master, he immediately set out to approach Kozan Mongo, the abbot of Kenchoji in Kamakura. It was March 1358, and Bassui was now thirty-one. Perhaps because he was dissatisfied somehow with the easy confirmation he received from Kozan, Bassui chose that moment to don Buddhist robes and declare himself a traditional Zen monk. From this time forward, his life became an unending pilgrimage.

After tracking many miles, Bassui stopped at Horinji, a temple where he had high hopes of finding a true master, but he was so unimpressed by the famous Fukuan Soko, abbot in charge of two thousand disciples, that he returned to Tokukei and announced his intention to become a hermit. Tokukei claimed he detected a bit of arrogance in the decision and warned Bassui against isolating himself. "All right, then," said Bassui, "I'm your disciple." And he moved into his friend's hermitage for the next full year.

At Tokukei's recommendation, Bassui next set out to check his enlightenment experience with Koho Kakumyo at Unjuji in Izuma. Assured that he would find a truly great teacher this time, Bassui was optimistic. Koho was, after all, in the direct line of Dogen, who had brought Chinese Zen to Japan; and Koho's teacher had taken the precepts from Keizan Jokin, the third patriarch in the Japanese Soto Zen sect. Bassui was not disappointed. Koho, who was strict and uncompromising about both the Buddhist precepts and the practice of zazen, refused to confirm Bassui's realization unless he remained at Unjuji and formally declared himself a disciple. Irritated at being cornered this way, Bassui tried to strike a compromise: he would see Koho daily and sit zazen in the monastery, but he would do so as a commuter, living in a hut somewhere off the temple grounds. To his surprise, the great teacher, having detected a promising, if difficult, student, agreed, instructing Bassui to sit with the beginner's koan, Joshu's "Mu." (A monk asked Joshu, "Does a dog have buddha nature?" Joshu answered, *"Mu!"*)

In a morning interview, Koho asked, "What is *mu*?"

"Mountains, rivers, and the great earth, grass, trees, and the forests, all are *mu*," replied Bassui with some self-satisfaction at having solved the koan so quickly.

Suddenly Koho erupted in a shout. "Don't use your mind!"

These words prompted Bassui's deep and unmistakable realization. Finding himself drenched in sweat, it was, as he later described to a disciple, "as though I had lost my life root, like a barrel whose bottom had been smashed open." Groping to find his way out of the teacher's room, Bassui bumped his head. On the path leading back to his little hut, he was still so gripped by the experience of his *satori* that he had to grasp at the walls to keep from falling. When he finally arrived and threw himself down inside, he burst into tears.

The next evening's interview was almost as much of a shock, for even before Bassui had opened his mouth, Koho cried out, "My Dharma will not vanish. All may now be happy. My Dharma will not disappear!"

His enlightenment now true, and truly confirmed, Bassui replied with the following poem.

> Six windows naturally open, a cold lone flower,
> Unju [Koho] strikes the rubbish from my eyes,
> Crushes the gem in my hand right before me,
> So be it, this gold has become hard iron.

Nonetheless, without waiting to receive Koho's formal transmission, the restless wanderer took to the road again. At thirty-two, Bassui returned to his old hermitage to announce the good news. Tokukei, seeing that Bassui was truly ripe now, advised him to build his own hermitage and teach. Again following his old friend's advice, Bassui established himself a short distance away in his home province at Nanasawa.

Four years passed, and one night Bassui dreamed that Koho was about to die. Immediately, he set out on a return visit to Unjuji, where indeed he found his teacher gravely ill. But Bassui's relations with the other monks were so strained that conflicts quickly arose. After all, who was this tree-dwelling eccentric who refused to recite the sutras and insisted on special dispensation to live off monastery grounds? Why had he gotten such a quick and easy transmission? It did not take long for the nomadic Bassui to realize that he wasn't welcome, and he immediately lit out for another one of his temporary hermitages in the nearby province of Ki. On the way, he visited an acquaintance named Jikushitsu Genko, abbot of Eigenji, where he was so well received that he was even asked to deliver a formal Dharma talk. Being Bassui, he encouraged the monks to avoid monkish Zen and apply their realization in their actual lives rather than depending on formalized rituals, institutions, and hierarchy.

A true example of his own preaching, Bassui remained elusive, refusing many monastery posts, preferring to sit alone in small hermitages and temples, and secretly stealing away in the night as soon as too many disciples collected around him. For twenty years, from the age of thirty-two until he was fifty-two, he moved around Japan in this fashion, spending periods in various hermitages and visiting teachers. His Zen was portable, requiring no ritual or priestly formalities, no traditional koans, although he did work through *The Record of Rinzai* and *The Blue Cliff Record* koan collections with Chikugan Teizosu, a hermit monk with whom he studied for a time, and later used koans to illustrate his own teachings.

Inevitably, age caused Bassui to slow down, and, in 1378, he was forced to settle in a temple on Mount Takemori in Kai province. As soon as the word went out, Bassui found to his amazement that he had collected over eight hundred disciples! Reluctantly, he formally became a Zen teacher. Nevertheless, he was still so stubbornly antimonastic that he refused to call his temple a monastery, using the suffix *an* (temple) instead of *ji* (monastery) when naming it Kagaku-an. Here, at age fifty-four, with only seven years left to live, Bassui drew up thirty-three rules for the behavior of his disciples. It was an eccentric document, dispensing with the usual religious emphasis on lineage and ceremony in favor of zazen practiced in simple, hermetic style. He was, however, scathing in his attacks on drunkenness, prohibiting any of his monks from taking so much as a drop of alcohol. "The true meaning of the precepts," he declared enigmatically, "is that one should refrain not only from drinking alcohol but also from getting drunk on nirvana." Then, on one memorable occasion, he openly got drunk in front of all his students, and, when questioned about it, said it was to show them how not to get stuck on regulations!

Having been enlightened on hearing the sound of a mountain stream, Bassui identified strongly with the Buddhist archetype of the bodhisattva Kannon, one who hears the sounds of the world. Bassui therefore had a shrine erected to Kannon, indicating to his followers that he wished it to serve as his own burial place. On the twentieth of March, in 1387, he sat up straight, with legs crossed in zazen posture, and addressed his students in a loud voice: "Look directly! What is this? Look in this manner and you won't be fooled!" Again he repeated the phrase, and then passed away. True to his vow to save all beings, like Kannon herself, Bassui did not hold himself aloof from the muddy world, but spent the years after his enlightenment encouraging others to seek their true nature and be relieved of their suffering.

A Zen teacher who avoided all formal approaches to Zen, Bassui warned students not to indulge in koan practice before they had seen a bit into their own nature. Spontaneous in method, striving foremost to bring people to realization, he taught according to the capacity and temperament of the individual student, even recommending to those who were inclined to do so that copying down sutras was a good way to "empty the mind." Bassui even went so far as to encourage people to mount memorial services for the dead in order to give the deceased a chance for enlightenment as well. He used folklore and legend, and was not above throwing in a bit of superstition when necessary to prod his disciples into realization. All teachings were directed to a single point: namely, that seeing into one's original nature *is* buddhahood.

His rustic style is evident in the title of his recorded teachings, *Enzan Wadeigassui (A Collection of Mud and Water From Enzan)*, published in colloquial Japanese for the ordinary reader. Tirelessly, and in a variety of ways, he posed to his students the question that had brought him to his own enlightenment: "Who is the master that is hearing at this very moment?"

Bassui's gentle Crazy Cloud approach, his anarchistic bias, did not adapt itself to a formalized Zen lineage. He was to the very core a hermit monk, a reluctant reformer whose own distaste for the ceremonial trappings associated with Zen led him to follow a single-minded, individualistic path to realization. Quite spontaneously he came upon a universal question common to all children ("Who am I?") and forged it into a koan that continues to liberate those who would follow it through anywhere and anytime. Bassui's zazen is the method of looking into the mind, of asking continuously whether sleeping, waking, or working, "What is my own mind? Who is it that sees colors, hears sounds, moves the limbs of my body? What is this mind that has no color, sex, or distinction of any kind, is unborn and undying, yet reflects countless thoughts and images like a mirror?" He assures his students that no buddha or bodhisattva can penetrate this question for them, that it is like a child being hurt in a dream, crying for its parent to rescue it. The parent would love nothing more than to come to its aid, to stop its suffering, but only by waking itself will the child be free of the painful dream. Deep and constant questioning, he says, is sure to break the delusory fiction we call our "self," revealing that "Mind is itself Buddha."

Again and again he urges his students to return to the question, even after they have had some realization. "Cast off what has been realized," he tells them, "turn back to the subject that realizes, to the root bottom, and resolutely go on." Still further, even after attaining deep insight, Bassui exhorts the seeker to polish realization until "it positively illumines the entire universe." To those who do not attain *satori* in this lifetime, but continue meditating in this fashion, he promises realization in the next life, comparing their hard work to preparation for a journey in advance, with an easy outcome as soon as the traveler embarks.

When asked what to do about thoughts, Bassui told his disciples to accept them as transient unreality and go on asking, "What is this mind?" or "Who is hearing these sounds?" Alluding to Kannon as his archetypal model for penetrating the essential self through sound, he prepared the listener for experiences of "emptiness," for encountering a great Void: "Do not mistake this state for self-realization," he warned, "but continue to ask yourself even more intensely, 'What is it that hears?'" Presently, the voidness will disappear, giving way to total darkness. Still, he enjoins the student, keep on asking relentlessly, "What is it that hears?" Even the serenity obtained through zazen is illusory, Bassui maintains, nothing but a transient reflection. "You must advance beyond the stage where your reason is of any avail"—to discover the all-embracing mind that does not come into existence with the body or die with the body's destruction, yet suffuses every act of seeing, hearing, smelling, speaking, moving.

Like all Zen reformers, Bassui emphasized experience over ceremony and traditional forms of religious worship. Yet he was more tolerant than most in his handling of students who were not yet ready to abandon the timeworn sutras or to give up petitioning the savior buddhas. Sutras, he told them, were helpful if they focused the mind away from ruminating thoughts; so were koans, or memorial services for that matter. But all these were only "fingers pointing to the moon, and not the moon itself." The last refuge for those wishing to discover themselves was the experience of one's own mind, the very foundation for every koan, buddha, and sutra. "If you catch even a glimpse of your self-nature," he promised, "it is the same as reading and understanding all the sutras simultaneously, none excepted, without so much as holding one in your hand and reading a word." To prepare for the experience, one could use bowing before the Buddha as a preliminary exercise, what he called "horizontalizing the mast of ego." But Bassui advised against fasting and other ascetic practices, claiming that the practice of Zen was purification enough. He chided students who sought visionary experiences, saying that wanting to be different from "ordinary" people was as much a delusion as any other distracting thought. "Don't involve yourself in such fantasies but only inquire: 'What is the master who sees all this?'"

He used certain traditional Zen koans for individual students, presumably after they had shown some penetration of his preliminary, "Who is the master that is hearing this sound?" A favorite case from the *Mumonkan (The Gateless Gate)*—in which the sixth Zen patriarch comes upon two monks arguing over a flag moving in the wind, one saying it is the wind that moves, the other saying it is the flag, with the patriarch assuring them both that it is their minds that are moving—provided Bassui with a useful barometer for measuring the degree of his student's insight. Another koan—in which Zen master Baso replies to the Layman P'ang's question "What kind of man is it that has no companion among the ten thousand things?" with "I'll tell you after you've drunk up the waters of the West River in one gulp!"—also appears in Bassui's exchanges with students on more than one occasion. But he relied most often on his own natural koan, "Who is hearing?" as the surefire means to self-realization. "Your physical being doesn't hear, nor does the void. Then what does? Strive to find out. Put aside your rational intellect, give up all techniques....Just get rid of the notion of self."

Bassui was very psychological in his approach to self-realization. He alluded always to the cognitive process of blending subject and object. His method stressed mental reflection on the subject rather than the sensory approach emphasized by a teacher like Bankei, for example. Bassui worked almost exclusively by means of questioning—"Who is it that hears, sees, walks?"—a method that lends itself as comfortably to today's psychologically oriented Western Zen practitioner as it did to the large lay audience of his own day. The question-and-answer, or public Dharma combat mode found in his *Collection of Mud and Water from Enzan* provides us with a very clear model of his approach. When a lay student asks how Zen, with its koans and records of old masters, can be considered a teaching "outside the scriptures," Bassui cries out: "Layman!" When the man responds, "Yes?" Bassui asks, "From which teachings did that yes come?" The layman, getting the point, lowers his head and bows.

Bassui continues to address the audience: "When you decide to come here, you do so by yourself. When you want to ask a question, you do it by yourself. You do not depend on another nor do you use the teachings of the Buddha.... Clever worldly statements, the written word, reason and duty, discrimination and understanding cannot reach this Zen." He warns further that those who use scripture and formal religious teaching aren't necessarily enlightened either, and that Zen monks who are ignorant of scripture aren't all deeply realized. Nonetheless, neither Buddha nor scriptures should stand in the way of perceiving that which is there from the beginning in the completeness and perfection of every being. "The leg and arm movements of a newborn baby are also the splendid work of buddha nature...so is the flying bird, the running hare, the scudding cloud. So too is the very conversation we are having right now." The difference between the Zen practitioner and the scriptural Buddhist is that the former lives by direct experience of the Buddha and the latter is like someone who sees another person hit by an arrow and stands there talking about it from the sidelines.

To those with questions about the ethical precepts of Buddhism apart from direct Zen experience, Bassui says that the *paramitas* all boil down to seeing into your own buddha nature. Anger, attachment, and the rest are all telescoped into the one peak experience of glimpsing the reality of the hearer, seer, walker, sleeper, lover, hater, and so on. For people fascinated with the supernatural gifts that are supposedly attained through deep meditation, Bassui has this to say: "Wise men consider physical manifestations of supernatural powers a karmic hindrance.... They are the results of attachment to drugs and charms, the evil deeds of demons and heretics and the powers of delusion." Similarly, he interprets all traditional religious injunctions metaphorically: fasting thus becomes looking into one's own nature and cutting off delusion; when literally practiced, however, fasting is nothing more than heresy. Breaking the precepts is living by the deluded mind, and seeing into one's true nature is keeping them all perfectly. The other approach, guarding the precepts, or working from without, can be a "shortcut for entering the buddha gate" when it is used for meditating on "Who is it that keeps the precepts?"

Several students came to Bassui with the practice of calling on the names of savior buddhas like Jizo. With great patience, he explained to them that *ji* means "earth" and *zo* means "storehouse," or mind nature. Then he urged them to "realize that all the names of the bodhisattvas are just different names for the nature of the Mind.... Ordinary people, being unaware of this truth, become attached to the names, and, in the hope of attaining buddhahood, seek the Buddha and Dharma outside of their minds. It's like cooking sand in the hope of producing rice." The

Jizo metaphor shows that "the true nature of the Dharma body of ordinary people is everywhere teaching of the many creations that come from it." Bassui extended this even further, adding that all the sermons of all the buddhas are only metaphors pointing to the minds of ordinary people. Thus he made no distinctions whatsoever between laypeople and monks, telling his mixed audiences that those teachers who did so were preaching fallacious doctrine that would "lead to hell." Bassui's Zen was strictly nonsectarian, embracing even non-Buddhists and social outcasts. For him, seeing into original nature was synonymous with the highest form of religious practice. Meditation did not require one to be a Buddhist, or a man, or an ascetic. Buddha, he argued, did not gain buddhahood from reading and reciting sutras, but from meditating.

Bassui challenged Zen monks to cite the exact records prescribing designated periods for religious services, stating that these customs only dated back to the time of the Mongol invasion of Japan, when the ruling house commanded prayer services. "The more I think about it," he added, "these...periods of religious service were not prayers, but simply the result of a decline in the Buddha Way and the Royal Way." Then he enjoined his monks not to waste time on such matters, but to cut off everything and practice zazen. In keeping with his iconoclasm, Bassui reinterpreted all the traditional religious practices of his time: sutra study, ceremonies, buddha worship, and the search for salvation through miracles. He divested zazen of all cultural, superstitious, and social accretions, sometimes with gentle irony. "Reciting part of a sutra with the desire to benefit others is like reciting a recipe in the hope it will prevent people from starving." To a culture steeped in religious superstition and worship of authority, such teaching may have appeared blasphemous. Nonetheless, thousands of spiritual seekers came to hear him assure them that the voices of frogs and worms, the sound of wind and raindrops, were all speaking the wonderful language of the Dharma.

Bassui was the most encouraging of Zen teachers. Instead of browbeating his students into realization, he coaxed and led them. Students who complained of no results were assured that continued meditation would bring them further along in their karmic preparation for self-realization. Some, he said, were sharp and quick, others more gradual. Yet all minds could be applied universally; everyone could see colors with their eyes, hear sounds with their ears, smell with their noses, have discussions with their mouths, and feel with their skins. This made them all buddhas. Most important, students were to have faith in themselves rather than in miraculous shrines or in lineage charts, or in ascetic practices that included burning the body, or in aggressive question-and-answer combat. He warned against becoming obsessed with one koan or precept, and scolded students who arrogantly criticized and condemned other Zen practitioners. He kept a careful check on disciples who evidenced a predilection for occult practices, and knocked others out of their stuporous trances. Fanatical moralists and hedonists were both "sick in mind" as far as he was concerned, and he urged serious Zen students to avoid such people. He likened all such extreme behavior to notorious robbers whose overlord was the conscious mind, "the pit of knowledge based on attachment to form."

How to conquer this notorious band of ruffians? "Just stop your wandering, look penetratingly into your inherent nature, and, concentrating your spiritual energy, sit in zazen and break through." No expedient means are necessary in Bassui's Zen. All it takes is a quick look at the one who is reading this right now. Who is that one?

4

Ikkyu: The Emperor of Renegades

The Muromachi period (1338–1573), which saw Japan's artistic renaissance as well as its most devastating starvation, plagues, and riots, served as a fittingly tumultuous backdrop for the life of Ikkyu, Japan's most popular and controversial genius, a man the critic R.H. Blyth called "the greatest Zen monk in Japan." By the time Ikkyu was born in 1394, the warring factions that had split the government in two—the northern court in Kyoto, and the southern court at Yoshino—had been forged into an uneasy and ever-volatile coexistence under the powerful warrior shogun Ashikaga Takauji. Loyal to the line of the late emperor Go-daigo, the southern faction continued to resist Ashikaga rule until 1392, when a compromise rulership agreement was reached—though never practiced. In 1272, in order to avoid disputes over his line of succession, Emperor Go-saga had introduced a royal edict implementing alternating succession drawn from the descendants of his second and seventh sons. Instead of ensuring the emperor's line, however, the plan created even greater disputes and questions of succession that resulted in over one hundred years of factional strife. By 1392, Go-komatsu, a pawn of the victorious strongman Ashikaga Takauji, became the legitimate one-hundredth emperor of Japan for both southern and northern parties. Ruling in name only, Go-komatsu served as a convenient national figurehead for the real powerholders, the Ashikaga shoguns of the house of Hosokawa.

The religious, political, and economic shifts in these most terrible and vital years not only directly parallel the Zen monk Ikkyu's life, personality, and teachings, but they are virtually the stuff of his own history. For Ikkyu was the illegitimate son of Emperor Go-komatsu himself and thus a dangerous potential heir to the throne after his mother, a concubine sent as a peace gift by the southern Yoshino faction, was pushed out of favor by a northern rival and driven from court to raise her infant son in secret.

Japan in the fifteenth century was in many ways as mobile, open, violent, and economically shifting as it was in the twentieth. Trade flourished, great merchant ships plied the seas, bringing with them a developing currency economy and modernized farming methods, making overnight fortunes for rice brokers and usurers, and opening the way for roving armies and mercenaries ready to plunge into war at any slight, both real and imaginary. From the Chinese mainland came art and Buddhist philosophy—especially the Rinzai form of Zen associated with the "manly" discipline expected of the powerful ruling samurai class. The shogun leadership, or Hojo, established the Five Mountain temple hierarchy known as *gozan* in imitation of the contemporary Chinese temple system, where, in exchange for patronage, the monks would provide culture and Buddhism to the brutal warrior class. The *gozan* were structured around Kyoto, the capital associated with the Ashikaga shogunate, and soon pushed into the background the more esoteric and elaborate Tendai and Shingon forms of Buddhism that had been favored by the emperors. Several hundred state temples comprised the *gozan* system, where religious advancement included paying fees in high places and competing for bureaucratic influence. Zen abbots in major temples like Nanzenji in Kyoto functioned more as tutors, advisers, diplomats, businessmen, poets, and artists than they did as clergymen. Zen Buddhism, in this bluntly commercial-military fashion, thus became the hallmark of the ruling warrior class.

The emperor Go-daigo had made Daitokuji in Kyoto the "place of imperial worship" in 1333. His successor Go-hanazono patronized Myoshinji, only a few miles distant, thereby initiating a second strain of Zen that, in Ikkyu's time, came to rival its parent temple. The original school, before it split under the influence of the shogunate (who favored Myoshinji and therefore pressed Daitokuji into the background) was known as Otokan Zen, an acronym referring to its three founding fathers, Daio, Daito, and Kanzan. It was to these founding fathers, Daio and Daito in particular, that Ikkyu looked for a "pure" Zen that surpassed all imperial boundaries, a Zen practiced in the manner of Daio Kokushi (1235–1309), who brought the lineage directly from China's Kido Chigu (Hsü-t'ang Chih-yü), and passed it on to his successor Daito Kokushi (1282–1337). Daito, after receiving *inka* (the seal of approval and acknowledgment of enlightenment) from his teacher, established himself in a rundown hut outside of Kyoto. With his handful of disciples, he spent seven obscure years earning his keep among the beggars occupying the mudflats under the Gojo bridge. Daito brought Zen out of the court and into the streets, thereby creating a popular version of the sect that was to influence every aspect of art and culture of the period. Called back by the emperor Go-daigo as abbot of the temple named in his honor, Daito reluctantly returned to clerical life—

as Ikkyu, his Dharma heir, was to do over a hundred years later—and became "teacher of the nation."

By the fifteenth century, the struggle between the imperially sponsored Daitokuji and the shogunate's chief temple, Nanzenji, had encompassed Myoshinji as well. The spirituality in the monasteries, whether emperor-dominated or shogun-sponsored, was decayed. Many priests sold *inka*, or seals of enlightenment, to wealthy donors, and some spent less time training novices in meditation than in shaving their eyebrows, powdering their faces, dressing them in women's clothing, and forcing them into carnal acts. Brewing and drinking sake, writing elegant Chinese poetry to order, teaching calligraphy to shoguns, and attending lavish banquets took up the time of the Muromachi Zen masters.

Only a few subtemples scattered mostly on the outskirts of the capital, poor and shabby dwellings maintained by Otokan diehards, upheld the spiritual discipline of devoted Zen meditation, thereby contributing to the continuation of the Buddhadharma. It was in two such subtemples that Ikkyu would receive his spiritual training.

Ikkyu was born on New Year's Day 1394, in Saga, an out-of-the-way suburb of Kyoto where aristocrats who no longer enjoyed the favors of court were quietly retired. Forced by her enemies to leave her seventeen-year-old lover, emperor Go-komatsu, Ikkyu's pregnant mother had retreated to a mansion in Saga, happy to have been spared her life. The baby was raised by servants and was permanently separated from his mother at the age of five, when he was placed in Ankokuji, a nearby Rinzai Zen temple, to keep him from any identification with future political aspirations and thus save him from assassination. It was not unusual for aristocrats of the

Muromachi period to place their sons in Zen temples, for they functioned as the "finishing schools" of an era in which priests held the key to high culture. As a monk, Ikkyu could blend in with the other boys of his class and survive even as the emperor's illegitimate son.

The curriculum at Ankokuji consisted of training in Chinese language and culture, the paragon of attainment in high Japanese circles. Typically, Ikkyu's Ankokuji masters spent more time in teaching literary and artistic subjects than in training their shaven-headed novices to meditate. *Gozan* Zen was so popular, in fact, that the shogun himself had his head shaved and was ordained as a Zen priest.

As a novice, the illegitimate son of the emperor received the name Shuken; it was not until nineteen years later that he became Ikkyu, One Pause, the name conferred upon him by his master Kaso as a confirmation of enlightenment.

The boy Shuken proved to be a born musician and poet. From his priest-teachers he learned the elegant forms of Chinese poetry, art, literature, and appeared, from his early imitations of Chinese lyrics, to be headed for the typical life of a *gozan* priest. Unlike the other temple boys, however, Ikkyu had no family to speak of. He was kept strictly isolated from his mother, consoling himself by turning out sad verses about ancient Chinese concubines who had found disfavor at court and suffered exile. Moreover, he was physically unattractive, with a squat, rectangular face, unaristo-cratic pug nose, and doleful eyes. His intellectual brilliance had to make up for his common features and rumored heritage.

At thirteen, Ikkyu moved to Kenninji, the oldest Zen temple in Kyoto, to study under Botetsu, a priest famous for his out-standing scholarship and poetic instruction. As one of the five highest-ranking temples of the Ashikaga shogunate, Kenninji was fiercely competitive, filled with the best budding young poet-priests of the day. Here Ikkyu wrote his adolescent versions of T'ang dynasty poetry, even managing to get a volume of verse into print. But it was here, too, in the very seat of power and political influence, that Ikkyu's religious nonconformism burst forth. Soon his teenage poetry of plum blossoms and waning moons gave way to biting criticism of the Kenninji hierarchy, attacking the temple for its worldly pursuits, its lack of spiritual training, its snobbish class distinctions among monks, its emphasis on politics over enlightenment. On his own, Ikkyu doggedly sat zazen until he could no longer endure the Kenninji environment and, in the fall of 1410, he moved to Mibu, a temple headed by the abbot Seiso, a Confucian specialist and chanting master. This short-lived stay proving equally unbearable, the young Ikkyu moved once again—this time out of the powerful *gozan* system to an obscure temple on the shores of Lake Biwa, where he found himself to be the single disciple of Keno, Modest Old Man, abbot of Saikinji, Temple of Western Gold. This shabby temple, with its lone disciplinarian master who refused to give written *inka*, at last provided Ikkyu with the brand of Rinzai Zen he'd been longing for.

Rinzai's refusal to accept *inka* from Obaku, his master, and Keno's refusal to grant it appealed as much to the reformer in Ikkyu as it did to the renegade. After all, weren't *inka* being bought and sold in the *gozan* marketplace along with patronage? Keno's example, and Rinzai's before him, exerted such a powerful influence on Ikkyu's mind that he never accepted or gave *inka* throughout his life as a Zen student or teacher. For the legitimate heir of Rinzai, true Zen meant transmission beyond words, scriptures, or written certificates of enlightenment. And Keno was just such a master—unconventional, uncompromising, strict in his dedication to meditation, with no worldly ambitions whatsoever. Ikkyu spent four years training in the lonely Temple of Western Gold, until Keno's sudden death put an end to his Zen idyll.

In December of 1414, the twenty-year-old Ikkyu fasted and performed the funeral rites alone for the old priest who had had no other disciples. For seven days, Ikkyu carried out his religious duties, then, in a condition of shock, hunger, and despair, he attempted to drown himself in Lake Biwa. Like his choice of Keno as his Zen teacher, this first suicide attempt shows the uncompromising, emotional, even excessively self-dramatizing side of Ikkyu's nature. Later, as a venerated Zen master himself, he would not hesitate to try suicide again in public protest over what he saw as the shogun's attempt to destroy his Zen lineage and ruin the nation. Both suicide attempts were, coincidentally, aborted by the timely intervention of the royal family. At the Lake Biwa shore it was his mother's messenger, sent to follow the distraught young monk, who saved him with her plea to go on living for her sake. In his public "fast to the death" when he was fifty-three, it was his father's successor, his cousin Go-hanazono, whose imperial decree prevented his death. From the first, Ikkyu was not one to hide his emotions, his weaknesses, and his character flaws. His scathing criticism could be turned against the corrupt religious hierarchy in one moment and, with equal intensity, leveled upon himself in a violent suicidal gesture a moment later.

Desperate for enlightenment, Ikkyu set out to find a new teacher. He had heard of another severe, incorruptible old Zen disciplinarian, a master named Kaso who headed a branch temple of Daitokuji, also located on Lake Biwa, the fateful site of

Ikkyu's attempted suicide, and what was to be his eventual Great Death *(satori)* experience six years later.

Kaso's temple, Zenko-an, was no less rundown than Keno's had been. He, too, hated the corruption of the capital and refused repeated offers of high position in the Daitokuji hierarchy. But Kaso at least had a few monks studying with him, and one nun. His head monk, Yoso, a man of twenty years' training, acted as chief disciplinarian, and in keeping with true Zen tradition on greeting new applicants, poured a bucket of slop water on Ikkyu's head when he appeared at the temple gate. Undeterred, Ikkyu waited outside for three days, while a reluctant Kaso pondered whether to accept a novice who had only recently attempted suicide and—on top of that—was rumored to be the emperor's illegitimate son. On the fourth day he relented, welcoming Ikkyu into the most Spartan of Zen temples, where novice and teacher alike worked in the biting cold until hands bled and icicles formed on their blankets.

For nine years, Ikkyu struggled with his assigned koans, meditating on them every day, then facing Kaso morning and evening in private interviews and answering checking questions that either confirmed or denied his penetration of the koan. Characterizing the painful process of his deepening insight, Ikkyu wrote in a poem: "I suffer the pains of Hell." In summer he meditated alone on Lake Biwa in a little boat loaned to him by a fisherman friend. His artistic gifts were turned to doll making in a Kyoto shop, where he spent as long as a month earning money for the temple. In his sparse free moments, he would mingle with the wild, poor fortunetellers, wine merchants, prostitutes, and fishermen who comprised the citizenry of Katada, the town surrounding Zenko-an.

As a musician and poet, Ikkyu's first enlightenment experience not surprisingly came through sound. In 1418, he was working on Case 15 of the *Mumonkan*, "Tozan's Sixty Blows." In the koan, Tozan Ryokai (Tung-shan Liang-chieh) comes to see the great master Unmon (Yü-men Wen-yen), who asks him several "ordinary" questions like "Where have you come from?" and "Where have you trained during the summer?" and so forth. Tozan gives straightforward answers and is told, "I spare you sixty blows." When he returns the next day, he asks Unmon where he was at fault in calling down the master's wrath. Unmon says, "You rice bag! Do you wander around west of the river, south of the lake?" And Tozan experiences great *satori*.

One day a troupe of blind singers stopped at Zenko-an to perform a popular ballad of tragic love. As he was listening to the performance, Ikkyu suddenly penetrated the Tozan koan. His experience was confirmed in his formal interview with Kaso, and he was given the Dharma name *Ikkyu*, One Pause, to commemorate the "single moment" insight he had attained. In response, Ikkyu wrote a poem.

> From the world of passions,
> > returning to the world of passions.
> There is a moment's pause—
> > if it rains, let it rain,
> If the wind blows, let it blow.

Then, in the summer of 1420, as he was sitting in his little boat on Lake Biwa engaged in meditation, again a sound provoked an awakening—at the cawing of a crow in early evening, Ikkyu achieved his great *satori*. The entire universe became the cawing of the crow, and even "One Pause" dropped away. Kaso confirmed the *satori*, tested him further with checking questions, and said, "This is the answer of an *arhat*, but not yet a Zen master."

"So I'm an *arhat*," Ikkyu replied. "I don't need to be a Zen master."

With that, Kaso cried, "Ah, so you really are a Zen master after all!" and immediately wrote out a certificate of *inka*. Ikkyu took the certificate, promptly threw it to the ground, then turned and left the room.

When head monk Yoso got word of Ikkyu's behavior, he became enraged. A serious Zen student for twenty years, he had to endure not only the great enlightenment of this impudent twenty-six-year-old intruder, but to suffer his scorn of the most coveted seal in Zen circles. For his own part, Yoso had treasured a portrait of Kaso as a "symbolic" seal of *his* insight and Dharma succession, but, on seeing him show it around, Kaso dashed his hopes by shouting, "If you ever call this scroll *inka*, I'll burn it!" Ikkyu's arrogance only added salt to Yoso's wounds, and the two soon became bitter enemies. Each man tried to show his loyalty to the teacher in his own way. When Kaso grew ill with dysentery, Ikkyu, whose enlightenment only served to develop his bizarre style of expression, cleaned the excrement with his hands. Yoso and the other disciples used brooms and sticks. When confronted by Yoso for his strange show of devotion, Ikkyu replied, "Since it is the dirt of our master I must not dislike it."

Increasingly, Ikkyu's behavior began to irritate not only Yoso, but Kaso as well. When lay patrons visited, the young monk would blurt out insults like, "Zen isn't a matter of fashion," and stalk out of the room. He also leveled many open attacks against the stylish life in Zenko-an's parent temple, Daitokuji, and publicly excoriated the "phony monks in cow skirts" at a memorial feast he attended there. Finally, his unorthodox behavior among the townspeople of Katada, his drunken revels, and his mockery of Zen rites of succession proved too much even for the unconventional Kaso, who, in 1423, gave Yoso *inka* and made him his formal Dharma heir. Ikkyu's response was immediate and typical. He left the monastery for a life of wandering, turning up every now and then at Daitokuji ceremonies in the patched robe and straw sandals of a mendicant. When admonished by Kaso for his rude appearance, Ikkyu quoted Rinzai, saying, "Do not hold on to robes," and walked off. Recognizing Ikkyu's genius beneath his anarchist's guise, a hapless Kaso replied later that day to the question of who would be his successor: "It will be the mad one." Kaso's spiritual preference for an heir was the "mad" Ikkyu, but when the old master died, it was Yoso—the "cultivated one"—who became abbot of Daitokuji.

Ikkyu wandered about in the spirit of his beloved idols Rinzai and Daito, characterizing himself in his poems as Kyoun, Crazy Cloud—a pun on the "cloud" prefix constituting the traditional word for monk, *unsui*, or "cloud-water," and pointing to his singularly "crazy" form of Zen. Unlike his predecessors, whose pilgrimage years were relatively brief, Ikkyu's footloose wanderings lasted from the time he was twenty-nine to the age of fifty-seven. Unlike Rinzai and Daito, too, Ikkyu refused to take up the formal role of a Zen master or the abbotship of a temple. Somewhere in his wanderings, though, Ikkyu managed to attract a handful of like-minded eccentrics, as well as a wife and son. *The Chronicle of the Japanese Monk Ikkyu*, a year-by-year account of his life, reportedly documented by his major disciple Bokusai, describes Ikkyu's circle as students made "of stern stuff, able to forget bodily comforts for the sake of the Dharma. They gathered dry sticks for firewood and scooped drinking water from the torrents…. They were diligent and untiring." In a ramshackle dwelling named the Hut of the Blind Donkey in honor of Rinzai's appellation for his successors, Ikkyu settled down to teach, by his own life's example, Rinzai's exhortation to "shit and piss and just be ordinary." When his wife died, he took his son as a disciple into his Blind Donkey temple, with its broken walls and rotten ridgepole. This was no dubious honor, for Ikkyu refused admittance to anyone who came for anything but serious Zen study.

Ikkyu continued to write his seditious, muckraking poems against usurious Zen temples and their rich and powerful overlords. He took up the cause of the hardpressed farmers and townspeople, whom he counted among his students, writing during one of the many citizens' uprisings demanding cancellation of debts from the Hosokawa shoguns:

> Robbers never strike poor houses.
> One man's wealth is not wealth for the whole country.
> I believe that calamity has its origin in good fortune.
> You lose your soul over a hundred thousand pieces of
> copper.

In 1425, Yoshikaza, the newly appointed shogun, died of alcoholism, and his retired father Yoshimochi had to resume the position again. Yoshimochi was himself so mentally deranged by alcoholism that he could not rule and gave way to a successor who was soon assassinated. In the midst of this social breakdown, Ikkyu fearlessly criticized not only the corruption of Zen, but the political situation as well. In a collection of openly seditious Crazy Cloud poems, he wrote:

> Greed for luxuries, for rice and money undermines
>   the imperial palace.
> It is not good that I even think about beautiful
>   women when all Japan is in an extremely
>   deplorable condition.
> This one retainer has his heart in shreds!

Unable to hide from the terrible realities of daily life in Muromachi Japan, he assumed the nonmonastic life of a layman, eating meat and fish, drinking wine, making love to women, and celebrating them in his poems. As a living example of Rinzai's dictum to avoid "loving the sacred and hating the secular," Ikkyu sought to bring true Zen practice out of the monastery and into the street, where, like Daito before him, he felt it belonged. Striking out openly against the dissolute Rinzai Zen institutions in the capital, he developed the persona of the mad monk to enforce his message that "it is easy to enter the realm of the buddhas. Much harder to enter the world of demons." So far, he had trained for more than fifteen years in the conventional, strict, and "manly" style of Zen; now he was determined to "enter the marketplace with bliss-bestowing hands," mingling with ordinary people, living as ordinary people lived, and thereby preaching the Dharma in whatever unconventional forms it might take.

Unlike Rinzai, however, Ikkyu was not a fierce and physically violent man, but a lover, a poet who could memorialize a pet sparrow and write tenderly about the beauty of women while at the same time trashing the Zen establishment. Though the rough-and-tumble *Record of Rinzai* was his bible (he even went so far as to memorize it), Ikkyu translated Rinzai's teaching through the highly sensitive vessel of his own nature and experience. And though he imitated Rinzai physically by growing a beard and long hair while still remaining a monk, Ikkyu departed from Rinzai's "masculine" Zen style, including women as his students, Dharma companions, and social and intellectual equals. Indeed, in a society where the ruling samurai flaunted their misogyny in their preference for the love of young boys, Ikkyu's "feminist" views alone were enough to label him mad. It was in the brothels and geisha houses that he developed his Red Thread Zen, a notion he borrowed from the old Chinese master Kido, and extended to deep and subtle levels of realization in "this very body" as the "Lotus of the true law," linking human beings to birth and death by the red thread of passion, and its resulting bloody umbilicus. Closely related to tantric Buddhism, which used sexual union as a religious ritual, Ikkyu's Red Thread form of Zen practice was the most radical non-dualist interpretation of the sexual act proposed by any Zen master before or since.

By encouraging such worldly varieties of Zen practice, Ikkyu developed an entirely new aesthetic in the process, creating new forms of calligraphy, poetry, Noh theater, tea ceremony, and ceramics. His "running" calligraphic style and *kyo*, or "crazy," even sometimes pornographic poetry were expanded by his lay students, many of whom were leading painters, actors, and sculptors of the period. Among them was his son Jotei, who later became one of Japan's leading tea masters. Above all, Ikkyu cultivated a life of sparseness and poverty that resulted in the highly valued Japanese *wabi* ideal of stark simplicity, which characterizes that country's aesthetic even today.

His folksy religious style emerged with his move to Sakai, a boomtown along the banks of Lake Biwa, which, like Katada, was populated by ruffians, wandering women, pirates, wealthy merchants, and con artists—Ikkyu's ideal "congregants." In this atmosphere, accompanied by his little band of loyal monks and lay students, Ikkyu turned forty-one on New Year's Day of 1435. Instead of preaching a traditional New Year's Day sermon, however, he woke early and rushed out into the city streets, brandishing a long wooden sword and smacking the hilt to call the people to attention. According to Bokusai's *Chronicle*, the puzzled townspeople gathered, crying, "What use does a monk have for a sword? Swords are used for killing!" To which Ikkyu replied: "You don't know it yet, but these days the world is full of a false wisdom that is just like this wooden sword. As long as it is kept in the scabbard, it looks as good as a real blade, but if it is drawn out from the scabbard, it is seen to be only a sliver of wood. It cannot even kill people—much less make them live!" The citizens of Sakai laughingly got the point and applauded their eccentric priest. Ikkyu felt that he alone held the great sword of Bodhisattva Manjushri, the blade of wisdom that cuts all delusion and grants realization.

Yet despite his outward "madness," by all evidence, Ikkyu was a strict adherent to Rinzai's rigorous Zen; his demand for strong commitment to meditation and koan practice and formal interviews with an enlightened teacher formed the core of his own career. The setting may have been informal, his students more often laypeople than formally ordained monks, but his Zen practice was far more traditional than the ritualized business going on in the *gozan* temples. For ten disastrous days, he tried to perform as abbot of Nioi-an, a subtemple on the grounds of Daitokuji, when, prevailed upon by his followers to assume the position in honor of his beloved old teacher Kaso's memorial anniversary, he accepted Yoso's offer. At the memorial banquet, however, Yoso's wealthy guests made it clear that in exchange for large donations, they expected Ikkyu to sell them written *inka*. In the midst of the banquet, Ikkyu got up and stalked out, followed by his chief disciples Bokusai and Bokushitsu.

Drawing up an inventory of all the goods in the temple, he attached it to a poem that he hung on the wall as a declaration of his resignation.

> After ten days in this temple, my mind is spinning—
> The "red thread" of passion is very strong in my loins,
> If you wish to locate me another day,
> Look in the fish stall, the sake shop, or the brothel!

More likely, Ikkyu really spent the next month sitting in *sesshin* (meditation retreat) out in the fields of patron Shiten Shoiku's estate in the southern part of Kyoto with his disciples, giving Dharma talks and answering students' questions. His Zen was rendered directly, in face-to-face encounter. To organize his teaching and urge students on, he handed them each a scroll that said:

> I am a simple man and have not certified anyone during my lifetime; I fear that after my death there will be no one to speak for me. As I received my certification in private, I did not publicize the fact. But if a man takes it on himself to propagate the Dharma and starts his own sect in secret, the regulations will be disarrayed. Such men should be quickly reported

to the authorities and punished. They betray Buddhism and are my hated enemies. Important indeed is the protection of the Dharma. How could anyone stand to one side and look on with folded arms?

Ikkyu's upright insistence on the true expression of Daito's lineage even impressed two of Yoso's own Daitokuji monks, Tsu and Kin. Both men turned up at Ikkyu's shabby Sakai headquarters one day, asking to become his disciples, and Ikkyu greeted them warmly. But this did not stop Yoso from making one of his periodic false gestures of attempted reconciliation by inviting Ikkyu to a clerical feast. Bokusai records word for word the ironic, increasingly bitter exchange between the two old opponents, with Yoso appearing at the temple gate himself, shouting, "Your arrival is much delayed. I was about to send someone to bring you here. I wanted to inform you that you have hurled shit-water in Kaso's face…"

Ikkyu replied calmly, "You needn't play the filial brother with me. Kindly clarify what you mean by 'throwing shit-water.'"

Yoso then went on to accuse Ikkyu of using the Daitokuji lineage and reciting the Dharma lectures of its masters for his own ulterior motives.

Ikkyu retorted, "I, on the other hand, hear that you extol the false practice of leaving off *sanzen* interviews with your disciples. *That* is what Kaso never heard of…. What other way could there be? How could there be anything without the interviews? No, it is you who throws shit-water. But into your own face. You cannot smear Kaso with your errors."

Growing angrier, Yoso sputtered, "I carry his certificate. By what right do you insult me?"

"I was also certified," said Ikkyu, "though such things are not for public comparisons."

"Well, I suppose I have no way to *prove* that you *were not* certified."

At that, Ikkyu gave a great laugh and walked off.

But then, in 1447, Ikkyu and Yoso had to join forces to save their beloved lineage from being overtaken by the Hosokawa shoguns, who, as patrons of Myoshinji, had always managed to push the imperially aligned Daitokuji into the background. As the great ruling powers in Japan at the time, the Hosokawas pressured the emperor to grant Daitokuji's chief abbotship to a Myoshinji rival. This provoked a rebellion in Daitokuji that resulted in the suicide of one priest and the imprisonment of several others. In open protest, Ikkyu embarked on a hunger strike out in the mountains surrounding Kyoto, writing:

> I am ashamed to be still among the living;
> So many years have I studied Zen and practiced the
>   Way, yet now heavy problems.
> Indeed, the Buddhist Truth seems to have disappeared.
> In its place, the King of Demons rises a hundred
>   feet tall!

As Kaso's legitimate heir, even the hated Yoso was preferable to a *gozan*-appointed interloper in the Daitokuji lineage. As he sat in the midst of a thunderstorm, growing weak with hunger, Ikkyu was approached by an imperial messenger of his cousin, Go-hanazono.

"If the reverend monk continues to do thus, the Buddha's Way and the Imperial Way will perish! How can he cause such? How can the master desert his country at this time?" the emperor pleaded. Ikkyu had made his point. He gave up the fast, and Daitokuji was saved—with Yoso as abbot, and Ikkyu wandering, as much the "crazy cloud" as before.

By 1457 the Hosokawas had so drained the population economically that the helpless masses erupted in civil war. Troops representing all sides looted and burned whole sections of Kyoto, including Ikkyu's city headquarters at the Hut of the Blind Donkey. So he and his friends moved south to the country. With the Onin War flaring around them and all the grand palaces and monasteries razed, Ikkyu's band felt lucky to be spared and thus gratefully named their temple Thank You Hermitage.

People died by the thousands; at one point the streets of Kyoto were obstructed by animal and human corpses of those who had starved or died of plague. Still, the shoguns and their Rinzai priests enjoyed an economic heyday. Ikkyu's response to the display of greed, hatred, and ignorance was a religious allegory he called *Skeletons*. This macabre treatise on death, which could barely equal the actual misery and slaughter around him, prescribed an antidote to the hellish events in its enjoiner to "concentrate wholly on zazen." Everyday life, even at its worst, could not be separated from true Zen practice. Thus, meditation in Ikkyu's country hermitage continued in the midst of the war. It was here, too, that his disciple Zenchiko developed Noh theater, and that the tea ceremony reached its apex as a meditative form. Ikkyu continued to write his stinging criticisms of temple and state, reproaching "the arrogant strong who continue to play music and enjoy life even though the whole populace is suffering," and published a series of bilious outpourings against Yoso and other public figures under the ironic title *Self Criticisms*.

As Ikkyu entered his seventies, he also embarked upon a period of passionate companionship that was to last into his eighties. In 1471, Lady Shin, a blind singer, composer, and skilled musician, entered the circle of Zen-inspired musicians, painters, and poets at Thank You Hermitage and changed Ikkyu's life. The old Zen master was seventy-seven, his mistress in her late thirties. All we know about the romance is what Ikkyu leaves us in his graphic and informative poetry celebrating their love. Bokusai's *Chronicle* remains mute on the topic, but he did manage to execute an amazing official portrait of Ikkyu, commissioned by the master himself, which includes the blind woman singer. This *chinzo*, or Zen portrait, still hanging in Daitokuji today, depicts Ikkyu minus the usual priest's staff, wearing plain monk's garb. He is painted in a grey, empty circle denoting the essential emptiness of things, while Lady Shin, seated below, dressed in professional finery and playing her *koto*, represents the manifest world of form.

In Lady Shin, or Mori, Ikkyu finally located his own missing female self. Unashamedly, he praised her brilliance and celebrated her gifts in his writing and in their public life together. Moreover, Ikkyu incorporated bold elements of their physical relationship into his teaching of Zen, playing on koans in an erotic context that bound the manifest and essential worlds in a loveknot. Thus, in Ikkyu's interpretation, the koan "In what ways do my hands resemble the Buddha's hands?" given by Oryo (Huang-lung Hui-nan), an eleventh-century Rinzai master, becomes:

Calling My Hand Mori's Hand
My hand, how it resembles Mori's hand.
I believe the lady is the master of loveplay; If I get ill,
    she can cure the jeweled stem.
And then they rejoice, the monks at my meeting.

This and other radical restatements of Zen methods and formalities of practice honoring woman and the Red Thread that binds even the most enlightened of Zen masters to passion, birth, and death, celebrate Ikkyu's joy in human love. References to himself as Mukei, the "dream boudoir" monk, indicate that in sexuality there lies a profoundly sacred spiritual practice.

> Who carries on the basic tradition of the Rinzai sect?
> The ultimate blackness of annihilation, the three principles [of Zen] exist at the "Hut of the Blind Donkey."
> This old priest "Dream-Boudoir" on his moon-
> viewing pavilion,
> Night after night leads a poetic life, over-drinking.

It was Lady Shin, Dharma companion and poetic inspiration, who permitted the "old priest" deeper and deeper insight into "the basic tradition of the Rinzai sect."

In 1474, Go-tsuchimikado, the reigning emperor, commanded Ikkyu to become abbot of Daitokuji. Kyoto was in ruins as a result of the Onin War, and there was literally no Daitokuji to house the new abbot. Ikkyu, now in his eighties, was given the task of rebuilding it from scratch. The throne itself was reduced to such poverty that the imperial retainers had to sell court treasures in exchange for rice. Only Ikkyu's powerfully wealthy merchant patrons, the newly emerged economic victors of the wars, were sufficiently solvent to assume the task of restoring their master's home temple. With characteristic zeal for his beloved lineage, Ikkyu not only agreed to discharge the impossible request, but, on accepting it, enacted a typically surrealistic Crazy Cloud founding ceremony. On a hilltop banking his tiny, obscure Sakai temple, he recited a strange series of poems accompanied by mimelike gestures representing the yet-to-be-built Daitokuji structures on their vacant "sites."

"The one remaining 'light' of Daito's school has been destroyed," he chanted. "How to explain the heart's singing the eternity of all? This priest who for fifty years wore only a straw raincoat and hat, today, shamefully, is a purple-robed abbot."

Without help from either the emperor or shogun, Ikkyu managed to rebuild. One disciple in particular, a Sakai merchant named Owa Sorin, even went so far as to fell the wooden masts of his ocean-going ships to support the roof of the new Daitokuji doctrine hall. By 1481, reconstruction was complete, and Ikkyu was dead. The errant monk who had tossed aside his *inka*, and with it all credentials as legal heir to Daito and Kaso's lineage, resurrected that lineage, then left it forever with no living link but a scroll-painted credo that read:

After my death, among my disciples will be those who will go to the forests or to the mountains (to meditate), and some may drink sake and enjoy women, but those disciples who lecture to an audience (and make money that way), talking about Zen as "the moral way," these men misappropriate Buddhism and are, in reality, Ikkyu's enemies (and not his followers).

They shall be punished by (the spirit) of Kaso, because they will be like a one-eyed man leading the blind. I never gave an inka to a single student, so if anyone boasts (of having one), he is not of the Ikkyu school. And if such a person claims that he understands Buddhism, summon the officials! Again I entreat you, thus can you show loyalty to me. Please think upon this message.

Like Saint Francis of Assisi, Ikkyu was celebrated at his death as much for his public acts of compassion as for his teachings, for making no distinctions between rich and poor, prostitutes and courtiers, the illustrious and the despised. Bokusai's *Chronicle* describes a monk followed by children who played with his beard, a man so gentle that birds would eat out of his hand; nevertheless, Ikkyu "hated the kind of Zen that was spooned out by masters who treated their disciples like so many pet birds." With his students, he was "strict and demanding." Detecting a lukewarm petitioner, he excused himself from teaching, saying, "I'm only a feeble old man," but with a sincere Zen student "he could do all sorts of things and demonstrate all kinds of abilities. He could expound both the profound truths and the evidence for them.... He was a surpassing man, with the essential character and deportment of the Buddha and the patriarchs."

Ikkyu's love for his Zen lineage convinced him to devote his last years to rebuilding the temple whose hierarchy he had spent most of his life demolishing in his writings and ridiculing with his antics. It is no coincidence that he chose Rinzai as his model, for the fierce "action Zen" of the old Chinese master six centuries before had also been a rebellion against the caste-dominated restrictions imposed upon it by a post-Confucian court. Emulating Rinzai's outspokenness, assuming his anticlerical beard, and refusing to shave his head, Ikkyu, the emperor's son, immersed himself in the masses, blurring class barriers of every kind, blasting the corrupt clerical establishment in his poetry and communicating his vast religious insight in extravagant symbols that, to Western minds, will immediately recall William Blake in England and Walt Whitman in America. Like them, too, he loved nature, extolled physical love, and used his art and spiritual vision to criticize the

moribund institutions of his time with incisive humor. He spoke
to the heart and senses, rather than to the samurai's power center
at the gut, the kind of Zen that fueled the practice of his day.
And he infused Zen for the first time with a feminine element
that it had long missed.

Ikkyu's poetic gifts were useful teaching tools, particularly
when applied to the traditional koan practice associated with
Rinzai Zen. By indulging in a more intimate form of Zen dialogue with his students—like the *renga*, or open-ended, witty
poetic repartee perfected by his disciple, poet Socho—Ikkyu har-
vested his own unique *mondo* (Zen dialogue) style, interpolating
direct allusions to the ancients into the immediate experience of
his circle. Thus, a night of drinking and poetry becomes:

> Men in the midst of their drunkenness, what can they
>   do about their wine-soaked guts?
> Sober, at the limit of their resources, they suck the
>   dregs.
> The lament of he who embraced the sands and cast
>   himself in the river by Hsiang-nan
> Draws out of this Crazy Cloud a laugh.

This poem includes an allusion to the Chinese official Ch'u
Yuan, who, though virtuous, found himself slandered by enemies.
In his dialogue with a fisherman at the shore of the lake where
he stood contemplating suicide, Ch'u Yuan said, "All the world is
muddied in confusion, only I am pure! All men are drunk, and I
alone am sober," an unenlightened man's parody of the Buddha's
enlightened exclamation, "Above the heavens, below the heavens,
only I, alone, and sacred."

The fisherman rejoined, "A true sage does not stick at mere things.... If all the world is a muddy turbulence, why do you not follow its current and rise upon its waves? If all men are drunk, why do you not drain their dregs and swill their thin wine with them?"

But Ch'u Yuan was too wrapped up in dualistic concepts of virtue and vice to heed the fisherman's Zen advice, and, composing a poem called "Embracing the Sands," he jumped into the river and drowned.

Ikkyu's use of this allusion to perfect Confucian virtue in a setting of his own "drunken" Zen teaching not only echoes the fisherman's words, but *lives* them. His poem, pregnant with Zen possibilities, itself becomes a multileveled koan for his students to consider, a stage for questions of right and wrong, drunkenness and sobriety, virtue and vice. The laugh of the Crazy Cloud is a succinct emblem uniting form and emptiness, delusion and enlightenment.

Ikkyu's life with Lady Shin exemplified Mahayana Buddhism in its tantric sexual forms, indicating that nirvana and this very world of human love and suffering are one and the same, that this very body is the Buddha. His popular forms of Zen practice brought meditation to laypeople in everyday life activities like cooking, farming, creating art, or caring for children. It suited the newly growing population of "lay monks" who gathered around him, people who were dedicated to Zen, but in the context of secular life outside the monasteries. Ikkyu taught and lived his brand of Rinzai's "action Zen" on the most human level. Secularizing it even further than Rinzai did, he used passionate, even shocking imagery and language to get his point across.

Skirting the dangerous wrath of the shogunate, he was highly critical of the religious authorities over which the government exerted direct control. Even as he overthrew the monastic forms and structures, his poetry and commitment to the *practice* of Zen show that he was profoundly religious and profoundly democratic, in the most spiritual and political sense of the word. Nothing could confine the individual once he or she was free of dualism. Moreover, no earthly power had the right to inhibit individual freedom either.

Ikkyu's *furyu*, or "far out" Zen, is that of Hotei, the bodhisattva of the marketplace with his candy-filled knapsack for children and his "bliss-bestowing hands." Radical in its non-dualism, this form of Zen Buddhism includes the entire universe in its realization and is not confined to the traditionally holy or sacred realms. If, as the Buddha discovered, all beings have buddha nature and are perfect just as they are, then liberation is not a matter of style and etiquette, but a living experience. Ikkyu's mentors Keno and Kaso felt that austere training, suited for a few very devoted seekers, would most likely bring about this deep realization. Ikkyu never denied their method, and his example of following this way closely for more than fifteen years until he reached great realization shows his esteem for his masters. But as an enlightened individual, standing on his own feet, he could not help but respond to the call of suffering all around him, and he went out into the world to ameliorate it. Hell and heaven, priest and layman, high and low, brilliant and stupid were equally sacred to Ikkyu in being "just this." With no concept of ultimate truth behind things, not even the concept of emptiness, he cut the link to the anguish and suffering that characterize the person beset by duality. Yet Ikkyu never denied his "ordinariness." He gloried in the world and celebrated it with the song of the divine fool.

5

Bankei: The Popular Preacher

When Bankei was eleven, he was so dissatisfied with the priest's answers to his searching spiritual questions that he hid in a small village shrine and stuffed his mouth full of poisonous spiders. This eccentric, fortunately unsuccessful, suicide attempt marks the beginning of Bankei's unique and fearless Zen pilgrimage.

He was born in 1622, the same year the third Tokugawa shogun Iemitsu took power and inaugurated one of the most repressive and autocratic regimes Japan had ever seen; he died in 1693, five years after Tsunayoshi, the fifth Tokugawa shogun, had ushered in the Genroku period, a loose, corrupt new order led by a recently emerged bourgeoisie. Like the times he lived in, Bankei's personality and religious style often expressed themselves in extremes. Take for example, the powerful Bakufu shogunate that, in a sixty-year span, expelled all foreigners from Japan, quelled a rebellion by forbidding all Japanese from traveling abroad, and so centralized governmental power as to paralyze individual landowners, village chieftains, farmers, and townspeople in a bureaucratic web that held even the imperial court a ceremonial prisoner. All major traffic routes throughout the country were closed off by barriers to keep would-be travelers and potential conspirators at home, and

the government, now centralized in Edo, made sure that no
bridges were constructed to make it easy to get to the capital.
Since Bankei was a popular preacher, an anarchist in a feudal dictatorship, it is all the more amazing that he managed to come and
go as he pleased in this impassable network of spies and border-
guards, that he gathered large, socially mixed audiences and
preached some very antiestablishment Zen in the bargain.

The paranoid seclusion policy that dominated most of the
Tokugawa period was a response to a strong and successful mis-
sionary campaign led largely by Portuguese Jesuits and Francis-
cans who had also managed to insinuate themselves into Japanese
politics. So pervasive was the Christian influence in seventeenth-
century Asia that China, Korea, and Vietnam followed the Japanese example and restricted all cultural and trading ties with the
West as well. The rigid physical strictures laid in place by the
Bakufu officials were no more suffocating than the social scene.
You were born into either a samurai, peasant, artisan, or merchant
family, and there you remained. Individual samurai chieftains, or
daimyo, were of two types: hereditary (descendants of those warriors who had fought with the winning side under shogun Ieyasu
at the great battle of Sekigahara) and outsider (those who had
surrendered to join him). The outsiders were never trusted; punished with heavy taxes and held hostage in a system that required
them to live for a year at court at Edo and then forced them to
leave wives and vassals behind when they returned home, these
samurai loosed their frustrations on the peasants and townspeople occupying the next lower rung on the social ladder. Since
Iemitsu's Japan was a military dictatorship that permitted virtually any member of the warrior class unrestricted power over his
vassals, it was not uncommon for a samurai to "test" his sword on

the neck of any hapless victim who crossed his path. Bankei's sermons are in fact laced with references to pious travelers and violent samurai coming face to face in encounters of this sort.

The Bakufu constitution, a rigidly fixed document drafted by the early shogunate and reaffirmed by each new shogun on his succession, defined the samurai code in detail and maintained a strict Confucian know-your-place discipline over everyone else. The hereditary *daimyo* were richer than the emperor and held all the land, but so quickly was the economy being transferred from agriculture to trade, from country to city, that the heavily taxed outsider samurai soon found themselves poverty stricken. By 1637, a group of such masterless samurai from the Shimabura peninsula, seeing nothing to lose, converted to Christianity and started an unsuccessful rebellion that left thirty-seven thousand Japanese Christians dead. This single event sparked the closure of Japan to the West and resulted in a brutal persecution of Christians that lasted for almost fifty years.

The Shimabura rebellion only exacerbated Bakufu paranoia. Spies were posted everywhere in a chaotic administration that had no legal code, but depended on the capricious decisions of local Tokugawa-appointed magistrates. Street billboards assaulted the eye with their harangues on proper ethical behavior; children were warned to be loyal to parents, citizens were admonished about frugality and hard work, and members of all classes were warned to stick to their station in life. To drive the point home, all sorts of torture and hideous public forms of punishment were designed to maintain the shogun's idea of "law and order." This meant that a townsman or farmer would be beheaded, drawn and quartered, and his corpse hung up in the village square, as an example for the same misdemeanor that would cost a samurai only a few yen. It was as though every man, woman, child, animal, and resource was put on Japan's earth for the use and delight of its military. But by cutting off all trade with the West, the shogun had placed himself in a double bind: the demands of his large and idle warrior class could no longer be met by Japan's limited local supply of material resources.

Until the installation of the seclusion laws of 1638, wealth had been measured in rice. Peasants, called the "machines who produce rice for the samurai to swallow," were totally oppressed by their masters, who, in turn, were perennially in debt to the merchants who supplied them with hard goods. As the samurai transferred their financial burdens to the farmers, they succeeded in destroying the agricultural economy on which the country had rested for centuries, and unwittingly relayed the financial power to money brokers and rice traders, or *chonin*. This class of townspeople not only accommodated the insatiable demands of the samurai at high interest rates, but in the process developed the huge commercial centers that were to become Nagasaki, Edo (modern Tokyo), Osaka, and Sakai. Trade grew so fast that by the end of the seventeenth century, money had entirely replaced rice as a means of exchange.

Though still low on the social ladder, the despised *chonin* held all the financial power, leaving the samurai to hold sway over traditional arts like swordsmanship, Noh, tea, flower arranging, and Confucian philosophy, while the merchant class developed the Kabuki theater, the arts of wood-block printing, and prose fiction, and maintained popular forms of Buddhism that had been displaced by the Confucian aristocracy. It was this group of nouveau riche merchants who formed the bulk of Bankei's religious audience, for Zen in particular marked the distinction between the neo-Confucian intelligentsia, with its strict Tokugawa hierarchy, and the newly emerging populist bourgeoisie. Bankei's sometimes strident denunciations of hierarchical Zen, his attacks on time-worn institutions like monasticism, koan practice, official confirmation of enlightenment, sutra chanting, and even Dharma transmission, are perfectly appropriate to his socially shifting times and to the needs of his mixed audience. Even the samurai who came to listen to his down-home sermons were converted.

Spurred by his emphasis on homely everyday reality, on conducting one's affairs in the here and now, Bankei's pupils were increasingly drawn from a literate population of town dwellers more interested in the floating world of prostitutes and teahouses than in the Buddhist fleeting nature of existence. And he addressed them in their own language and voice.

Born on Buddha's birthday, 8 April 1622, in the small village of Hamada, into a samurai family that had come upon hard times, Bankei was the fourth of five sons, and one of nine children. With the help of a local samurai patron in better financial condition than he, his father had opened a medical practice in a nearby village. Then, when Bankei was ten, his father died, leaving his eldest son Masayasu to continue the practice. The family followed the typical Confucian religious line that characterized the Tokugawa period, but adhered in spirit to the Buddhist-inspired samurai code. Zen had been organized into an authoritarian esoteric sect supported by the shogun in his effort to root out Christianity, but it was essentially drained of its vigor by the time Bankei began his religious search at the age of eleven.

He was a bright and difficult boy who, though assertive and almost unmanageably independent, harbored such a terrible fear of death that the adults in his family could discipline him immediately by pretending to lie down and die. Sent to the typical Confucian rote-method learning school of the day, Bankei annoyed his calligraphy teacher by refusing to copy the same characters as everyone else, and called down the wrath of his older brother by playing hooky. When Masayasu tried to punish him by instructing the ferryman not to take him across the river dividing school from home, Bankei just plunged into the water and, gasping, walked across with his toes barely touching the muddy bottom.

The death of his father had provoked the boy's moody search for an answer to the puzzle of birth and death, to the point where even his learned teachers could not satisfy his penetrating philosophical questions. One day, hearing the Confucian dictum: "The way of great learning lies in clarifying bright virtue," Bankei asked, "What is bright virtue?" His teacher replied, "The intrinsic nature of good in each person." Dissatisfied, Bankei approached other teachers and got answers like, "fundamental nature," and "the ultimate truth of heaven." By now Bankei was driven wild with the desire to find and experience this "bright virtue" that, he instinctively believed, held the key to life and death. Seeing that the answers did not lie at school, he stopped attending classes altogether and was dismissed from the family home by his brother. At the age of twelve, already a passionate attender of sermons and lectures given by Confucian scholars and Buddhist priests, never missing a religious meeting for miles around, Bankei set out to find the meaning of "bright virtue."

Like Ikkyu, who was also cast away early from his mother's loving care, Bankei was passionately devoted to his mother all his life, vowing to share with her his religious quest and to liberate her once he had found an answer to his burning question. Later, when his mother, as a ninety-year-old nun who had become his disciple, died in his arms, Bankei remarked that he had not spent his life searching in vain, for he had seen his mother become enlightened as a result of his teaching.

Though banished from home, Bankei was lucky in his friendship with his father's patron Sukeshizu, who offered him a little hut in the woods behind his own property. The boy carved the words "practice hermitage" on a shingle, placed it outside the entrance door, and moved inside. When he was not sitting in contemplation of bright virtue, Bankei spent his time reciting the *nembutsu* at a nearby Shin Buddhist temple. By the time he was fifteen, he had enrolled in a Shingon temple, where he studied esoteric Buddhism in the hope of finding his answer. Buddhism, rather than Confucianism, seemed to offer the best way to enlightenment, but even here, Bankei discovered an empty ritual habit, a religion given to form and letter over living spiritual experience.

One Buddhist priest advised the boy that he might find what he was looking for in a Zen temple about twenty miles from Hamada in Ako, with a Rinzai priest named Umpo. It was in 1638, the very year that the shogun instituted his policy of seclusion, that Bankei walked to Zuioji and met his first Zen teacher. The seventy-year-old Umpo was heir to the same incorruptible Otokan lineage that the young Ikkyu had found in Kaso's shabby Katada temple two centuries before. On first interview, Bankei asked his "bright virtue" question and was told to go sit zazen and find the answer for himself. Typically impulsive, Bankei demanded to have his head shaved and to be ordained on the spot. Umpo obliged him, giving him the Dharma name

Yotaku—"long polishing of the mind gem." He was not to be called Bankei until the age of thirty, four years after his enlightenment, when he was installed as a Myoshinji Zen priest in Kyoto.

Umpo used traditional koan practice as only one of his teaching methods, preferring the "direct" approach of sitting meditation. Thus, Bankei sat on his question until he was nineteen, when, still unenlightened, he left on a pilgrimage in the hope of easing his mind on his own. Living in temples on the way, or in huts, but mostly sleeping out in the open, he wandered as far as Osaka, emulating the great Zen teachers of Umpo's lineage by spending several years with the beggars under the Gojo bridge in Kyoto.

The extremist boy, who, in his frustration at encountering death, had swallowed a mouthful of poisonous spiders, now developed into a fanatical ascetic, intent upon a life of hardship and privation as a means to solving his dilemma. In his own words:

I pressed myself without mercy, draining myself mentally and physically; at times I practiced deep in the mountains, in places completely cut off from all human contact. I fashioned primitive shelters out of paper, pulled that over me, and did zazen seated inside; sometimes I would make a small lean-to by putting up two walls of thick paper boards, and sit in solitary darkness inside, doing zazen, never lying down to rest even for a moment. Whenever I heard of some teacher who I thought might be able to give me advice, I went immediately to visit him. I lived that way for several years. There were few places in the country I did not set foot.

In 1645, four years after he had left Zuioji, he returned to Umpo, his question still unresolved. Tearfully, he approached his teacher with his sad report of failure. "It's your desire to find someone that keeps you from your goal," said Umpo. Bankei turned and set off once again on his wanderings. In a lonely hermitage in the countryside to the north of Ako, he resolved to carry out his meditation to the death. His ten-foot cell consisted of only one opening large enough for a peasant's arm to slip through a bowl of food twice a day. A second, smaller hole provided him with a privy, and he shut out all light and noise by plastering the door with mud. Sitting on the cold rock floor until his buttocks and thighs bled and festered, he often neglected the food that was passed in to him. Fighting against what he called "the demon of sleep," he splashed his face with cold water at the slightest hint of drowsiness. Still he remained unenlightened.

Finally, his body had become so weakened by his asceticism that he contracted tuberculosis and could not eat at all. Spitting up huge gobs of blood, Bankei resigned himself to dying where he sat. Suddenly he felt "a strange sensation" in his throat and spat a huge ball of bloody phlegm against the wall opposite. Watching it slide, Bankei was instantly enlightened with the realization that "all things are perfectly resolved in the Unborn." Fourteen years of relentless struggle were rewarded in a split second with the deep, keen, and immediate resolution of his question. And with it, his health and appetite were immediately restored. Gulping down the half-cooked rice his attendant had fixed for him, Bankei returned from his Great Death experience a transformed man. Later, while washing his face in a nearby stream, the scent of plum blossoms spurred yet another insight, further confirming his confrontation with that which was "unborn" and "undying." Returning to Umpo, Bankei's *satori* was confirmed, as the "marrow of Bodhidharma's bones." Then Umpo recommended that the young man visit the great Gudo Toshaku, the most renowned Zen master of the day, for a further confirmation of his enlightenment experience.

At the time of Bankei's *satori,* Zen was a fossilized remnant of the two preceding centuries. Rinzai and Soto schools were in a constant "dialogue"—rivalry, really—over the best way to restore a living practice. Both were clearly aware that what passed for koans had degenerated into the mere parroting of venerable words in the mouths of unenlightened priests. Soto practitioners looked back to the writings of Dogen, the thirteenth-century founder of their sect, while the Rinzai school followed a strict Myoshinji line of koan Zen. Zen scholarship flourished—while Zen experience languished. Several nonconformist monks wandered about in search of enlightenment for themselves; eccentrics like Suzuki Shosan, an ex-samurai turned Zen priest; Ungo Kiyo; and Daigu Sochiku rejected the confirmation of their teachers as lifeless transmissions from old men who hadn't been enlightened themselves. Suzuki Shosan preached that work in the fields and wielding the sword in battle were sufficient practice. The other two wandered about teaching their own brand of Zen, confident in their enlightenment without formal transmission from anyone.

As a result of the Buddhist persecutions of the Ming dynasty, several Chinese refugee Zen teachers made their way to Japan, holding sway largely in Nagasaki, the only city permitted to foreigners. The two most famous Chinese Zen teachers among them, Dosha Chogen and Ingen Ryuki, both rejected by the Myoshinji-dominated Zen hierarchy, were such bitter rivals themselves that Ingen tried to have Dosha poisoned and ultimately succeeded in driving him back to China. Remaining as the sole "legitimate" Chinese Rinzai Zen master, Ingen stayed on in Japan to found a line of Obaku Zen that gathered many disciples and deeply influenced the arts of painting and calligraphy. Zen "reformers" were everywhere, but none could inject life into the practice.

The twenty-six-year-old Bankei took his place on the road alongside his fellow Zen pilgrims. Disappointed to hear that Gudo was away from his temple in Mino, Bankei tried other Zen teachers in Gifu province. To his disgust, he found that none of them could confirm his experience, for none of them were enlightened themselves! One kindly old priest even had the decency to admit this, urging Bankei to accept his own confirmation and not rely on the Zen writings of others.

For a year, Bankei lived in a series of hermitages in Gifu province until, in 1650, he returned to Harima, his hometown area, pondering how to teach the Buddha Way to others. In 1651, at Umpo's suggestion, he traveled to see the Chinese priest Dosha Chogen in Nagasaki. Begging his way across the Inland Sea, he crossed on a trading ship and, as soon as he landed, walked to the temple, Sofukuji, where the old Chinese master received him.

"You have penetrated through to the matter of the self. But you still have to clarify the matter beyond, which is the essence of our school," said Dosha. This qualified confirmation urging Bankei to take his *satori* out of the rarified realm of emptiness and put it to work in the world of ordinary life experience so miffed the young man that he turned and left without even making a bow of respect. But something in the old priest's words must have struck home, for Bankei remained at the temple and became Dosha's student, taking his place in the meditation hall along with the other monks. Though he could not communicate with his teacher in conversational Chinese, and Dosha understood no Japanese, Bankei managed to have interviews by means of written notes in formal Chinese. Still the rebel, Bankei refused, however, to go along with the Chinese-style monastic chanting and other foreign ritual practices. When Dosha reprimanded him for this, Bankei said, "The only reason I've come here at all is because I want to clarify the great matter. How can I afford to waste valuable time learning additional ways of chanting sutras?" Seeing what kind of monk he would have to put up with, Dosha let the matter rest, and made Bankei *tenzo*, monastery cook, for a year.

On the twenty-first of April in the year 1652, while sitting in the meditation hall, Bankei had another profound enlightenment experience. He rushed to Dosha's interview room and wrote, "What is the ultimate matter of Zen?"

"Whose matter?" was Dosha's written response.

Bankei held out his arms; Dosha was about to write again, but this time Bankei grabbed the brush and, tossing it to the floor, stalked out of the room.

Bankei's aloofness from the ritual practice and his cocksure attitude did not endear him to the other monks. Soon they were openly expressing their resentment of his special status with Dosha. The old teacher secretly advised Bankei to leave the temple for a while, which suited the nonconformist well enough. He returned to the Harima area, then moved on again to Yamato province near Nara, a remote place known for the abundance of hermit ascetics sprinkled among its hills. Here Bankei sat in a crudely fashioned hut, composing religious rainmaking songs for the peasants in return for food.

In 1653 he moved back to his own small hermitage in Mino province and continued deepening his realization in solitude.

From early on he had shown signs of psychic intuition, which, in 1653, during a particularly hard winter, disclosed to him that Umpo was ill. Several monks had gathered to sit with Bankei; one, a man named Sen, was especially dubious about Bankei's announcement that he would have to travel to see the sick Umpo. "How do you know that your teacher is ill? He is miles from here," Sen challenged him. Bankei confidently reiterated his intuition that Umpo was ill. Sen accused him of being a con man and laughingly offered to accompany him to prove the fraud.

Bankei accepted the challenge, and the two monks set out toward Ako. Halfway there, Bankei insisted on a detour, claiming that the wife of an old friend had just died in Osaka and that he was wanted there.

Again Sen cried "Fake!" as he hastened along after Bankei in the direction of Osaka. When they arrived at the friend's house, they were greeted by Bankei's friend, who was dressed in mourning clothes. "My wife died three days ago. Strange you should come now. She called your name during her final illness."

Bankei squared off with Sen, saying, "Am I such a con artist, then?" Sen's response was to swear allegiance to Bankei forever.

Such youthful displays of supernormal power were tempered in Bankei's middle life, however, for his reputation as a seer only hindered his efforts to teach people how to discover their basic unborn nature for themselves. Many ignorant and superstitious folk appeared at his sermons anyway in the hope of witnessing a miracle. Bankei's usual response was to turn their mind-reading requests back on them with humor.

When Bankei arrived at Zuioji on that trip, he was told that Umpo had died the night before, leaving instructions with his successor Bokuo Sogyu to encourage Bankei to teach. It was

1654, and Bankei had picked up five disciples in his wanderings. All accompanied him to Nagasaki to visit Dosha, who, meanwhile, was having his own political troubles with his Chinese rival Ingen. Always ready for a good fight, Bankei joined the Dosha faction and tried to gain the support of important patrons for his beleaguered teacher. Ingen's students stopped at nothing; they even burned Dosha's official transmission papers to make him "unfit" to teach Zen. When that didn't work, they resorted to still lower methods, which included the attempt at poisoning him. Bankei was off in Hirado in search of help from feudal lord Matsura Shigenobu, a powerful disciple of Dosha's, when the situation grew so bad that Dosha had to sail back to China in disgrace.

Matsura Shigenobu had become acquainted with Bankei when he was an anonymous monk begging in Edo. One of the lord's vassals overheard Bankei's comment at seeing a masterless horse tear through the streets out of control: "It is because master and horse are separate, not one." Sure that this could only be the remark of an "enlightened" Zen priest, Lord Shigenobu invited him to his home and eventually set him up as retreat master of the family temple in Hirado.

In 1658 Bankei was appointed Dharma heir of Umpo by Bokuo, the old teacher's primary successor. Now, as an official teacher in the Myoshinji line, Bankei could at last communicate his message about the Unborn in his unique and original fashion. As soon as the word was out, hordes began flocking to hear the riveting sermons of the iconoclastic reformer. For thirty-six years thereafter, Bankei would teach in temples, monasteries, meeting grounds, and at the estates of wealthy students. Most often accompanied on the road by his small band of full-time disciples, he roamed the length and breadth of the country preaching "unborn" Zen in his populist style. Three major temples sprang up to accommodate his two-month retreats: Ryumonji, built by a loyal childhood schoolmate who had become a wealthy shipowner in Bankei's hometown of Hamada; Nyohoji, in Ozu on the island of Shikoku; and Korinji in Edo. At first, Bankei tried sequestering himself with his small group of disciples at Nyohoji, intent on continuing to polish his realization and guide the others in his Heart-of-the-Matter Hermitage; but popular demand for his appearance in large public gatherings was so great that he was forced out into the open. Korinji, Bankei's Edo temple, built by *daimyo* Kyogoku Takatoyo at the specific request of his mother, a nun, was populated largely by powerful government bureaucrats, wealthy and not-so-wealthy samurai, retainers, and lower level aristocrats. Bankei's other two temples were in the country and therefore collected a more varied social assortment of monks, nuns, lay practitioners, fishermen, farmers, wealthy merchant upstarts, townsmen, and housewives, who sat out on the grass rapt at his words. By 1679, he was delivering sermons in over forty temples throughout Japan, maintaining a steady band of disciples on the road as he traveled. In Bankei's hands, the ailing Zen sect miraculously sprang to life in an entirely original form.

Bankei's small private retreats turned into huge *kessei*, two- and three-month intensive training periods held in winter and summer. Here, however, traditional meditation and personal koan interviews gave way to group practice, open question-and-answer sessions, and sometimes as many as three public talks a day. Unlike all other Zen temple *kessei*, Bankei's permitted no beating or scolding of students, no begging by the monks in his congregation, and no particular set schedule. Of the traditional forms, only periods for daily zazen and sutra chanting were held for those who wished to participate. As a Buddhist priest, Bankei himself continued to offer traditional ceremonies and private interviews, where, depending on the individual facing him, he gave advice on everything from personal family problems to koan practice. And he officiated at funerals, weddings, and Buddhist precept rituals as long as people asked for them.

Though he had no use for keeping formal records of his talks and forbade his students from doing so, Bankei's oral teachings were transmitted in the form of personal diaries and journals written by his closest disciples. One of these was a woman named Den Sutejo, an accomplished seventeenth-century poet who had married at seventeen, had six children, became a widow at forty, and, finally, a nun. From 1681 to 1696, when she died, Teikan, as Bankei named her, kept a diary documenting Bankei's travels, meetings, retreats, and illnesses, meticulously recording the types and numbers of people in attendance at every occasion. A famous entry occurs in 1690, when 1,680 clergymen and women—not to mention the throngs of laypeople who had come from as far north as Hokkaido and as far away as the Ryuku Islands—attended a winter retreat at Ryumonji, Bankei's home temple. So many appeared, in fact, writes Teikan, that the town's "barns, sheds, and storerooms" had to serve as sleeping quarters for the participants. In 1691, she reports, Bankei led a ninety-day winter retreat at Gyokuryuji in Mino for over six thousand people.

But Bankei's early ascetic practices had taken their toll on his health, and his teaching years were plagued by stomach spasms, coughs, and general collapses that forced him to retire for weeks at a time. By 1693 his health had so deteriorated that his disciples began building him a burial pagoda at Ryumonji. With their own funds and labor, laypeople, monks, samurai, rich and poor, peasants and townsfolk worked side by side day and night to complete the project. It was on a hot day on the tenth of August when Bankei was carried to Ryumonji on a litter. The next day, he told an attendant in secret that he would be dead within three months. For the time left to him, Bankei continued seeing students from his bed. Immediately before he died in November, as he'd predicted, he stopped taking food and medicine. Giving instructions to his most intimate students, he admonished them for their tears, saying, "How do you expect to see me, if you look at me in terms of birth and death?" When one disciple asked him to compose a traditional Zen death poem, he said:

I've lived for seventy-two years. I've been teaching people for forty-five. What I've been telling you and others every day during that time is all my death verse. I'm not going to make another one now, before I die, just because everyone else does it.

Bankei died peacefully at Ryumonji, and his ashes were divided between that temple and his Heart-of-the-Matter Hermitage at Nyohoji. Four hundred priests and 270 nuns were in attendance at his funeral; five thousand laypeople from every social class and rank came to honor their teacher. Forty-seven years after his death, though he had openly rejected the Zen hierarchy of his day by instituting his own populist form of practice, the government bestowed on him the greatest honor a Zen priest could attain, the title Kokushi, National Teacher.

What did Bankei teach? His *fusho* Zen, teaching the Unborn through sermons, and *hogo*, instruction, was anomalous even during the Tokugawa period when all sorts of footloose Zen men wandered about in the hope of reforming and reviving a dying practice. Moreover, it was dangerous during those days of persecution to preach anything foreign that could be even vaguely construed as "Christian." Yet his words cut through the dictatorial Confucian social codes designed to smother all individual thought and expression, reaching the ears and hearts of commoners and samurai, masters and servants, lay and clergy. His message was so simple that one did not have to be literate or a Buddhist to comprehend it. Bankei's teachings all boil down to letting go of all ideas and finding your own "unborn, original mind" right here and now without indulging in any particular religious discipline or belief. Though he remained loyal to Umpo and Dosha, he was quite open about their failings as Zen masters, even going so far as to tell his audience, "I can see now…that Dosha's realization was less than complete. If only he were alive today, I could make him into a fine teacher. It's a great shame. He died too soon." Bankei even turned himself into a figure of derision, urging his students to avoid following his own earlier misguided self-punishing example of Zen practice. The Unborn, he told them, is not something to be reached for or attained by discipline; it is not a condition of mind or religious ecstasy; it is right where you stand, perfect just as it is. All one need do to realize it is to be oneself, exactly as one is, doing exactly what one is doing, without commentary, self-consciousness, or judgment.

The mind is a mirror; thoughts rise and fall on it. There is no need to either hold or reject these thoughts, only to let them come and go. What keeps us from realizing this plain and essential truth about ourselves is our self-preoccupation and our acquired habit. Bankei's Zen is a process of deconditioning impulses and concepts that are accumulated from birth and frozen in memory. These impulses and concepts have led us into delusion about the real nature of ourselves and the world. The original mind from which we come forth is exchanged for these dualistic perceptions that cause us to be born into various states and conditions—human, beast, god—all psychological manifestations of anger, greed, and ignorance. The only way out of these perpetual "transmigrations" is by constantly returning to the Unborn in the experiential moment.

Unlike other Zen teachers with lay disciples, Bankei refused to rely on traditional modes for inducing realization of the Unborn, insisting instead that his listeners would catch a glimpse of it merely upon hearing his words. Rather than offering them meditation or koan practice, he used dialogue and exhortation, calling attention to the events of the immediate moment to shock, prod, and drive the questioner to experience the Unborn. Bankei himself was the vehicle; the daily life, problems, and situations of his students were the fuel. No one could say "that they have heard of anyone who has done this before me. I'm the first," Bankei told his audiences. He might have added that he was also the last, for when he died, his marvelous teaching gift died with him.

In working with individual students on specific questions of practice, he managed to touch on universal concerns. Anger, for example, became a medium for refining spiritual vision. When a farmer described his tendency to give way to fits of rage, Bankei responded:

You make yourself inwardly a first-class animal.... Therefore, you must thoroughly understand about *not* transforming the

Buddha-mind into other things.... Until you transform it, you live just as you are in the unborn Buddha-mind; you aren't deluded or unenlightened. The moment you do turn it into something else [like anger], you become an ignorant, deluded person.... By getting upset and favoring yourself you turn your Buddha-mind into a fighting spirit—and fall into a deluded existence of your own making.

Thus, in Bankei's Zen there is never a moment when we are not enlightened, only deluded by thoughts without substance that appear momentarily and disappear as soon as we disregard them. Consequently, Bankei never set aside a fixed time for "practice," saying:

When you're awake, you're awake in the same Buddha-mind you were sleeping in. You sleep in the Buddha-mind while you sleep and are up and about in the Buddha-mind while you're up and about. That way, you always stay in the Buddha-mind. You're never apart from it for an instant.... Now I don't urge people to sleep around here. But once they are asleep, you're making a serious mistake if you hit them....There's not a moment when you're not a Buddha.

Nonetheless, he conceded to the wishes of his students and allowed them to sit zazen when they wished to. His preferred approach, however, was to call attention to the sounds of the birds, dogs, bells, coughs, and breezes rustling the leaves of the trees as he talked. He illustrated the totally natural functioning of the Unborn in ordinary sense experience by daring his listeners to make a deliberate effort to hear the sounds, telling them, "You are able to hear and distinguish [them] when they occur without consciously intending to hear them because you're listening by means of the Unborn Buddha-mind." He denounced popular Zen techniques like raising a great ball of doubt in the mind, and, with tireless concentration, working on it until *satori* was attained. "You didn't have a doubt before, but now you're saddled with one," Bankei told a monk whose teacher had recommended such meditation. "You've turned your unborn mind into a ball of doubt, and that's absolutely wrong."

As a man who had experienced severe illness throughout his life, he was personally instructive to those who came with questions about how to endure physical suffering. The unborn mind is above and beyond pain or pleasure, he told them. Only with the arising of thought about illness and suffering does the Unborn assume the form of illness and suffering. Since it is perfectly human to moan when thoughts about illness cause us to submit to pain, it's best to just moan, and not put a martyr's face on it. The realized person, however, will be living in the Unborn whether sick or well, aware that it is the *thought* of sickness that is the cause of suffering.

Bankei suggested that anyone could try to recall the unborn mind without any other mindfulness practice or formal meditation.

Try to stay in the Unborn for thirty days. Once you've accustomed yourself to that, then you'll find it's impossible to live apart from the Unborn. It will come naturally to you then, and even if you don't want to, even if you grow tired of it, there'll still be no way you can avoid living in the Unborn and doing an admirable job of it too.

All it required was hearing, seeing, smelling, tasting, touching, breathing, living naturally in the world, going about one's business without one extraneous thought.

When approached by traditionalists who accused him of tossing out the venerable practice of koans, Bankei retorted that the great masters of the past had given living teachings face to face with their students; these dialogues and spontaneous exchanges had then ossified into rote methods irrelevant to the person who was standing right before him. How could we know, Bankei argued, if these intimate exchanges of long ago were helpful to us in our immediate situation? It was better to remain in the Unborn without creating extra work for ourselves.

To priests who regaled him with criticism for dispensing with rituals and precepts, Bankei replied by telling them that there was no distinction between observing and not observing these customs. Precepts were designed for evil-minded people; those who merely lived in the Unborn and weren't distracted from it by wicked thoughts and preoccupation with appearances had no use for them.

Questioners or challengers frequently gained realization in the moment of their public exchanges with him. In a dramatic reversal of tone and attitude, naysayers often became Bankei's students on the spot. Numerous cases like these perfectly illustrated to his listeners the premise of Bankei's assertion that only by listening to his words pointing directly to the unborn mind, without creating any particular thought or goal of transcending oneself, could realization come. The very act of listening was the Unborn revealing its mystery. He then urged his students to listen as many times as they could to his talks so as to make the experience familiar and keep from reverting to the old mental habit of clinging to distracting thoughts. His "method," he explained, was nothing more than remembering to lodge in the original unborn mind, which, unlike the body, was not created and was therefore indestructible even at the body's death. The Unborn only temporarily occupies this package of elements, allowing it to hear, smell, see, and physically experience the world. When these elements disintegrate, the unborn mind does not. Thus, there is no one without it, and no one can give it to you. Whether you farm, pray, trade, sing, or keep house, you are never without it. Nonetheless, he cautioned his enlightened students to continue penetrating the fathomless wisdom of the Unborn, for there is no end to it. This was his justification for refusing to confirm a "great *satori*," though he did declare Dairyo Sokyo as his successor. When Dairyo died two years before him, Bankei said, "I have lost both my arms." Without a formal successor, Bankei's lineage was doomed to die out.

Contrary to his wishes, Bankei's eighteenth-century Dharma heirs composed complicated classical Chinese collections of his teachings, adding exactly the kind of technical Buddhist jargon he abhorred and never used. Like so many other Crazy Cloud teachers after their deaths, Bankei, too, fell prey to well-meaning legend makers who perpetuated a form of Zen in his name that contradicted what he called his Clear-Eyed School.

Since Buddhist teaching at that time claimed that women could not gain enlightenment, many women appeared at Bankei's sermons to agonize over their evil fate. To them Bankei said:

Here's something that will prove to you that the Buddha-mind is the same in men and women…. Suppose that outside the temple walls someone started to beat on a drum or strike a bell. When you heard these sounds would the women here mistake the drumbeat for the bell, or the bell for the drumbeat? No. As far as hearing those sounds is concerned, no difference exists between the men and the women. It's not only true of men and women, there are people of all kinds in this hall: old people and young, priests and laity, and so on. But there wouldn't be any difference in the way that a young person, or a monk, or a layman heard the sounds either. The place in which there's no difference in the hearing of those sounds is the Unborn…and it's perfectly equal and absolutely the same in each one of you. When we say "This is a man," or "This is a woman," those are designations that result from the arising of thought. They come afterward. At the place of the Unborn, before the thought arises, attributes such as "man" or "woman" don't even exist.

This was tantamount to heresy for a society steeped in Confucian hierarchy, where women, like vassals and farm animals, were no more than the dumb property of their lords. The Unborn was the great equalizer. Even samurai could not avoid Bankei's pungent remarks. If anger could turn a farmer into an animal, then a cowardly or ignoble warrior was no better than a cur as well. He fascinated his audiences with stories about thieves turned monk, and violent monks turned thief, and rampaging samurai appeased by a moment's realization of the Unborn. He assuaged the fears of restless laypeople and clergy, telling them that their deluded effort to erase thoughts was like trying to "wash blood with blood." To would-be ascetics who denied that it was enough to listen to him to gain realization, he likened himself to a traveler who, finding himself and his tour group without water, made a long, hard climb up a mountain to fetch some. Then, bringing it back, he gave his thirsty companions a drink. What need for them now to make the same enervating climb?

> My own struggle was undertaken mistakenly, because I didn't happen to meet up with a clear-eyed master. Eventually, though, I discovered the Buddha-mind for myself. I have been telling others about theirs, so they'll know about it without going through that ordeal.

To philosophers and scholars who came to argue, Bankei dismissed the idea that reason or the discriminating intellect could bring enlightenment, for the very notion of seeking buddhahood distracted one from the Buddha-mind to begin with. It was impossible to become something that one already was. Similarly, he criticized those who believed that one could meditate oneself into *satori*, saying that meditation, or zazen, was itself nothing more than the Unborn doing peaceful sitting. Just sitting, just walking— nothing extraneous. His scorn for religious hocus-pocus poured out when a practitioner of the Shin (Nembutsu) sect claimed that Shinran, its founder, had pointed a writing brush at a piece of paper held across a river from where he stood and miraculously caused the six characters of Amida Buddha's name to appear on it. Laughing, Bankei replied that even mentioning such a person was like "putting dogs and men on an equal footing." It was better, he advised the *nembutsu* follower, to avoid cluttering up the mind with such nonsense by letting it function as a mirror that only reflected what passed in front of it and nothing more.

Like many Zen teachers, Bankei found that educated people had a particularly hard time grasping the Unborn in its simplicity.

Illiterate men and women were often much quicker at it, going right to the heart of the matter without a lot of ratiocination and questioning. Seekers who looked for the experience in books could only blind themselves, he said. Reading about it afterward in the sutras and writings of great Zen teachers was interesting only in that it confirmed what one had already found for oneself.

In one dramatic confrontation with a priest who had come to publicly debunk him, crying, "How can you save me when I don't accept your teaching?" Bankei only lifted his fan and asked the man to move forward a few steps. When the priest did so, Bankei asked him to come still further. The priest advanced, and Bankei said, "Look how well you accept it!" Vanquished, the debunker made a quick exit.

When asked how he fit into the line of great Zen teachers, Bankei replied, "Tokusan and Rinzai knew how to use the stick and shout; I know how to use the three inches [of my tongue]." He likened his golden-tongued teaching to a ball that had been smashed to bits and scattered among his listeners, each gaining a piece as large as his or her capacity to hold it. In the same vein, he condemned his contemporaries for making prisons of their monasteries, where even the smallest infraction resulted in corporal punishment and public humiliation. Bankei's simple, individually oriented Zen, his respect for the Unborn residing in all forms of life, had no place for the kind of "prying or bullying" that made students sick or resentful of the practice, or caused them to go mad.

The farmer for whom the "kaa kaa" of the crow and the "chuu-chuu" of the sparrow rang out the song of the Unborn was equal to Bankei himself. So too was the benighted monk who approached the master's chair and accused him of being "foolish."

"It's by being 'foolish' that the Tathagata saves sentient beings. To neither come nor go, but to remain as you innately are, without allowing the mind to become obscured—this is what's meant by Tathagata. And such was the way of all the patriarchs of the past," Bankei replied.

As he could not be insulted or put off by human challengers, Bankei could not be frightened even by wild animals. Once, when a wolf stood in his path, Bankei, noticing that the animal had a bone caught in its throat, walked up and dislodged it with his fingers. The wolf acknowledged its gratitude by wagging its tail; then it disappeared into the forest. But from that day on, whenever Bankei traveled along that particular road, the wolf would come bounding out in front of him and accompany him for a few miles toward his destination. To his fellow travelers Bankei had illustrated his own teaching in action: "Hesitate and it's lost; waver and it draws further and further away."

Though he refused to write an official death poem and was only privately a fine poet and talented painter and calligrapher, Bankei did leave his words behind in the sermons that were secretly recorded by his disciples and in the folk poetry he had written for the mountain farmers who kept him alive during his pilgrimage years. One such poem celebrating the New Year encompasses Bankei's entire teaching in his own unmistakable voice.

> What does it matter, the new year, the old year?
> I stretch out my legs and all alone have a quiet sleep
> Don't tell me the monks aren't getting their instruction
> Here and there the nightingale is singing; the high-
> est Zen.

6

Hakuin:
The Old Heretic under the Sala Tree

The child Iwajiro Nagasawa, who under his Buddhist name Hakuin Ekaku would become the great reformer of Japanese Rinzai Zen, was born on Christmas Day 1685, in the little town of Hara in the Japanese prefecture of Shizuoka. It was eight years before Bankei's death, a time that witnessed the overshadowing of Zen Buddhism by more popular forms like Nichiren and Shin. Buddhism itself had lost its primary position within Japanese religion to the Neo-Confucianism of scholars like Hayashi Razan, Kaibara Ekiken, and Tani Jichu, who excoriated the Buddhist doctrines of celibacy and retirement from the world as antisocial forces destructive of the cosmic order.

The glitter and glory of the reign of the first four Tokugawa shoguns, Ieyasu (1603–1616), Hidetada (1616–1622), Iemitsu (1622–1651), and Ietsuna (1651–1680), had worn off. The power and intelligence of these rulers, who had been surrounded by traditional, well-educated ministers and advisers, gave way to a short period of unrestrained fugitive pleasures and amusements. Theaters and restaurants, wrestling booths and "houses of joy," dwellings for countless actors, dancers, storytellers, jesters, courtesans, bathgirls, and dissolute samurai were centered mainly in the Bakufu capital of Edo. The new shogun Tsunayoshi, who triggered this short era of bourgeois frivolity and extravagance known as the Genroku (1688–1711), was a superstitious and spendthrift pedant. Defying his Confucian advisers, and neglecting their sound and sober politics, Tsunayoshi embarked on a campaign to renew the arts and education, and started an extensive building program in the capital. The exorbitant funding of these social and aesthetic reforms succeeded in devastating state finances, and the shogun's clumsy attempts to remedy the situation by enhancing the circulation of metal coinage in place of the traditional "rice currency," paired with draconian cuts in the salaries of retainers and a cut in the annual allowance for the imperial court in Kyoto, only led to an intolerable increase in food prices.

Oblivious to popular resentment and surrounding himself with small-minded advisers, Tsunayoshi extended his private sensibilities even further into the public domain by declaring the killing of animals a capital offense. This necessitated the creation of an enormous bureaucracy consisting of police and inspectors to keep track of all newborn litters and to make accurate lists of the sex and markings of the animals. Samurai who defied this decree were mercilessly put to death at the shogun's personal orders. Nicknaming him Inu-Kobo, or Dog-Shogun, the citizens of Edo did not grieve when Tsunayoshi was murdered by his wife in 1709.

Tsunayoshi's cultural bloom, with all its corrupt deviations, had come to an end. After six years of rule by his successors, two weak Tokugawa shoguns, a new strongman, Tokugawa Yoshimune (1716–1745), took power and reinforced the traditional samurai values of frugality, honor, and loyalty. As cultivated by the Yoshimune regime, this revival of earlier Tokugawa attitudes and values—particularly *bushido*, the "Way of the Warrior"—pervaded every aspect of Zen master Hakuin's life and teaching. Symbolizing samurai rejection of the new industrial and commercial wealth of the *chonin* (townspeople), *bushido* revived the freewheeling warrior spirit of the late sixteenth century, representing "the good old days," when power, loyalty, and the bravery of fighting warriors had not yet degenerated into apathy and when heroes could not be bought by the highest bidder. The spirit of *bushido* is best reflected in the book *Hagakure*, published around 1720, which contains the teachings of two elderly members of the samurai class, Yamamoto Tsunetomo and Tashiro Tsuramoto. These men tried to convey the truest spirit of the old-fashioned samurai by stressing the importance of the "art of dying." Absolute love and loyalty to one's deceased lord found its expression in the practice of *oibara*, joining him by committing ritual suicide, or *seppuku*. For Yoshimune warriors this was the romantic equivalent of dying together with one's lord on the battlefields of the past.

Bushido was nurtured by a misguided interpretation of Zen Buddhism that likened the fortitude and discipline of the warrior in battle to the Zen monk's singleminded concentration. Both disciplines focused on eliminating "worldly" thoughts and attaining a state of perfect serenity in the realization of the emptiness of all appearances. *Hagakure* author Yamamoto Tsunetomo himself became a Zen priest in his old age, preaching the perverse notion that humans are "like superbly contrived marionettes, who without strings attached, can strut, jump, and utter words on the stage of empty dreams."

Dovetailing with this warrior code, shogun Yoshimune inaugurated a powerful reaction against the fun-loving spirit of the

Genroku, which had undermined the samurai class and, by extension, the Bakufu government. In keeping with the spartan code of the samurai, he cut down on all state expenses, first and foremost on his own shogunal household expenditures, making it a point to dress in simple cotton garments and eat simple food. His policies were deliberately construed to hit the merchant class, especially in the capital at Edo, home to large numbers of government contractors and purveyors of luxury. Yoshimune passed laws prohibiting suits between samurai and merchants over loans, and townspeople were forbidden to assemble outside samurai houses to collect debts. But even these strict measures could not prevent the impoverishment of the warrior elite and a slow dissolution of the old class structure. By the time Yoshimune died, social dividing lines were so blurred that merchants could buy entry into the samurai class. Even the spirit of *bushido* had been appropriated by the *chonin*, who merged the traditional values of the warrior class with bourgeois notions of self-importance.

Paradoxically, however, Yoshimune also reopened the door to Western learning. Since the Exclusion Edicts of 1637, the only channel of communication with the West had been the little Dutch settlement at Nagasaki, and Japanese could learn of the outside world only through merchants and shipmasters. With the exception of Christian religious literature, Yoshimune lifted the ban on the importation of foreign books, and Western sciences like medicine and astronomy immediately began to penetrate Japanese life. Although Yoshimune appears to have been a man of considerable talents and some originality of mind, it is hard to understand why he undermined his own efforts to revive traditional samurai values by passing laws that indirectly benefited the merchant class. Perhaps as a follower of orthodox Confucianism, he was not willing to deprive himself of knowledge from other cultural sources. By bestowing his patronage upon Confucianists of various schools, he further weakened the influence of Buddhism, leaving the costs for the maintenance of temples and the priesthood to the individual *daimyos*, or feudal lords.

From the time of Yoshimune's death in 1745 to Hakuin's death in 1768, the country was frequently struck by plague and famine, the result of unbearable tax burdens and living conditions borne by the rural population. The life of the peasant had been constricted by fluctuating rice prices and a widening gap in living standard. Farmers, who were forced to borrow from moneylenders charging exorbitant interest rates, resorted to abortion and infanticide in order to keep families small enough to sustain what little was left after debts and taxes. This unbearable situation drove many farmers to desperate measures, and soon the countryside erupted in organized mass uprisings. Such riots were brutally quelled by government troops, killing thousands of male householders in the process and leaving many families to starve.

All efforts of the Bakufu government to regulate the price of rice, to fix rates of interest, and to annihilate outstanding samurai debts remained unsuccessful. In addition, a succession of incapable shoguns further weakened the government's hold on the country. The destruction of the old lifelong feudal relationship between lord and retainer, which had been based on loyalty rather than on cash, had progressed too far. The new wealthy merchant class and the moneylenders now controlled the economy of Japan. Slowly but surely, they changed the societal structure so thoroughly that, within a hundred years, the Tokugawa shogunate disappeared, giving way to the commercialization of power and the restoration of the imperial house of Meiji. It was against this transitional turn-of-the-century Japanese backdrop that Hakuin lived.

Iwajiro Nagasawa was the youngest son in a family of five children. His father and grandfather, though of high-class samurai birth, worked as postmasters in the little town of Hara, which, located in the immediate vicinity of Mount Fuji, served as a resting place for tired travelers on their way from the imperial capital, Kyoto, to the Bakufu capital, Edo, and back. His mother's family were devout followers of the *Lotus Sutra* sect (Nichiren), a form of Buddhism that Iwajiro would try to reform later on in his life.

Under the influence of his pious mother, Iwajiro soon began to show extraordinary talent for a religious life. When still a young boy, he expounded long sutra passages from memory, and meditated on the transitoriness of all things as he watched the passing clouds. Iwajiro, which means "boy of rock," quickly developed a strong body and an iron will. Biographical records describe a young man with a determined face and big, round, shining eyes. Hakuin later recalled himself as a fearless, impulsive fellow who delighted in catching and killing insects and small birds.

One day, his mother took him to a Nichiren sermon elucidating the agony of the eight burning hells. Iwajiro, close to physical breakdown, ran out of the temple, his body shaking with fear and terror for his sins. From that day on, the mere sight of a fire prompted long, uninterrupted musings about hell and its avoidance. To calm him, his mother taught him to recite certain passages from various Buddhist sutras and to invoke the name of the Shinto god Temman Tenjin. Impressed by the Buddhist sutras, Iwajiro soon started to test their effectiveness empirically. For several days he recited a sutra that was said to prevent the zealous follower from the harmful effects of fire and water. Taking a glowing iron from the hearth with his bare hand, Iwajiro painfully realized that he had made no progress on the path to purification. This experience convinced him that the only thing left to do was to become a monk, and he asked his parents for permission to enter a Zen monastery. After much pleading on his part and denial on theirs, Iwajiro finally got his way and was formally ordained at the age of fifteen. The abbot Tanrei Soden of Shoinji in his native Hara gave him the Buddhist name Ekaku, Crane of Wisdom. Soon after the ordination ceremony, Abbot Tanrei fell ill, and Ekaku was sent off to continue his Zen training with Abbot Sokudo of Daishoji in the nearby town of Numazu.

Disappointed by the stylistic approach to sutra study he found at the temple, Ekaku soon lost interest in his new surroundings and set out on a journey to find a "true teacher of Zen" who would bring him to *satori*. Now nineteen years old and physically very strong, Ekaku visited several temples, but found none of them satisfactory. During his travels he came across a biography of the Chinese T'ang period Zen master Ganto (Yen T'ou), famous for shouting so loudly at his assassination by bandits that he had been heard for miles around. Dismayed that such a distinguished Zen adept could still be touched by fear of death after devoting his life to the development of a pure and detached mind, Ekaku fell into doubt about the validity of his own quest. In this condition, he arrived at a little temple in the province of Mino, where Bao, a poor poet-monk who had collected a handful of disciples, was teaching the art of composing linked Zen verses in Chinese. For a time, Ekaku's inherent artistic talent overpowered the spiritual seeker in him, and he decided to remain with Bao.

But it was not long before his old fear of hell returned and drove him back to Zen.

One day, closing his eyes and invoking the aid of all the buddhas and ancestral teachers to guide his hands, Ekaku picked a book from Bao's library. To his delight he discovered that he had selected *Urging through the Zen Barriers*, a seventeenth-century collection of lectures and stories describing the rigorous practice of Chinese Zen masters. He opened the book at random and read about the famous Rinzai master Sekiso Keisho (Shih-shuang Ch'ing-shu), who, meditating day and night without interruption, had pierced his legs with a sharp wooden stick at the slightest hint of drowsiness. Ekaku's zeal was so aroused by Sekiso Keisho's example that, on hearing of his mother's death, he resolved to dedicate himself entirely to the realization of his buddha nature regardless of the consequences. Dispensing even with the obligatory funeral ceremonies for his mother, Ekaku left Bao's temple and resumed his spiritual search. At Joko monastery in Wakasa province, a lecture on the joy of realization so moved him that, with tears in his eyes, he decided to burn all his art work— including poems, calligraphies, and paintings—in the ultimate effort to devote his life exclusively to realizing the Unborn.

During his travels, Ekaku had begun to sit with Joshu's "Mu," the famous first koan of the thirteenth-century Chinese classic koan collection, *The Gateless Gate*:

A monk asked Joshu, "Does the dog have buddha nature or not?" Joshu said, "*Mu.*"

Mu literally means "nothing" or "no," but Joshu's answer is not a negation of the monk's question; instead, it reveals the quality of buddha nature in the spontaneity of the interaction. Combined with attention to the breath, *mu* is the meditation device that leads the student to *kensho*, a glimpse into his or her own buddha nature.

To resolve this ultimate question, Ekaku worked on *mu* with characteristic determination. When in the company of other traveling monks who had stopped to rest and admire the beautiful landscape, he would remain seated in zazen, murmuring, "What good is it to indulge in sensual pleasure when one's ultimate question is not yet resolved?" Once, when sitting in a temple shaken by earthquake during the 1707 eruption of Mount Fuji, Ekaku remained fixed on his cushion while all the other monks fled the meditation hall in a panic. A year later, at Eiganji in the province of Echigo, the twenty-four-year-old Ekaku was meditating assiduously day and night, sleeping only for minutes at a time. Suddenly, he was overcome by enormous tension manifesting itself in the form of a Great Doubt. This was followed by his first spiritual breakthrough, described later in a letter to an old Zen nun.

Suddenly a great doubt manifested itself before me. It was as though I were frozen solid in the midst of an ice sheet extending tens of thousands of miles. A purity filled my breast and I could neither go forward nor retreat. To all intents and purposes I was out of my mind and the "Mu" alone remained.... This state lasted for several days. Then I chanced to hear the sound of the temple bell and I was suddenly transformed. It was as if a sheet of ice had been smashed...and I returned to my senses. I felt that I had achieved the status of Ganto, who, through the three periods of time, encountered not the slightest loss [although he had been murdered by bandits]. All my former doubts vanished...and in a loud voice I called: "Wonderful, wonderful.

There is no cycle of birth and death through which one must pass. There is no enlightenment one must seek...." Smugly I thought to myself, "In the past two or three hundred years no one could have accomplished such a marvelous breakthrough as this."

The three crucial elements of the mystical experience are clearly discernible in this remarkable account of Ekaku's first *satori:* 1) *daigi*, the Great Doubt, a heightened tension connected with the strenuous effort of uninterrupted absorption in a state of single-minded focus on one's koan; 2) *daishi*, the Great Death, a sudden expansion of one's consciousness that includes the whole universe in the experience of body and mind dropping away; and 3) *daikangi*, the Great Joy, reemergence into the world of things with a fundamental understanding of nonseparateness accompanied by overwhelming love and joy.

Ekaku had finally reached his goal. Now eager to confirm his "huge" *satori*, he decided to get formal approval from the Zen masters. To his great disappointment, the teachers, who didn't regard his experience as anything more than a "small" *kensho*, refused to give him their seal of approval. Somewhat humbled, but still convinced of his enlightenment, Ekaku turned up at the little hermitage of Dokyo Etan, the Old Man of Shoju, a Zen master in his sixties who was as renowned for the depth of his Zen understanding as for his eccentricity.

Born into a samurai family, Dokyo had early developed a desire to become a monk. After a year of severe training with the famous Shido Bu'nan Zenji at his mountain hermitage, Dokyo experienced profound *satori* and received the seal of approval from his teacher. Still in his twenties, he resolved to follow the example of the eccentric Chinese T'ang dynasty monk Bokushu, and cut himself off from the world, sitting in deserted graveyards with wolves howling at his back, and finally retiring at the Shoju-an hermitage as the Old Man of Shoju.

In his first interview with the old hermit, Ekaku boasted of the "depth" and "clarity" of his own Zen understanding in the form of an elegant verse put down on a sheet of paper. Dokyo, crushing the paper with his left hand, held out his right hand and said, "Putting learning aside, what have you seen?"

"If I'd seen something I could present to you, I'd vomit it out," replied Ekaku, and, making a gagging sound, he pretended to vomit on Dokyo's hand

The old man came closer. "How do you understand Joshu's *mu?*" he tested the young monk.

"In Joshu's *mu* there is no place to put hands or feet," Ekaku replied, implicitly ridiculing the old man's outstretched hand.

Dokyo immediately grabbed Ekaku's nose, gave it a good twist, and laughed. "I found some place to put hands and feet!"

Nonplused, Ekaku conceded defeat and asked the hermit to tell him what was missing in his realization.

Dokyo assigned him a new koan. From that day on, at any sign of Ekaku's returning arrogance, the old man would reject his presentation by calling him a "poor hole-dwelling devil" to prod him out of his "emptiness addiction."

Taking up permanent residence at the hermitage, Ekaku mercilessly threw himself into long periods of uninterrupted meditation, only to be rejected and ridiculed by Dokyo time and again. Long painful weeks passed and nothing happened. The young monk felt he would rather die than leave the place without Dokyo's approval. His physical strength diminished, and, forcing himself beyond even his powerful endurance, Ekaku virtually stopped eating and sleeping. One day, on a trip to a nearby village while begging for food, Ekaku encountered a man who fiercely despised begging monks. Chasing Ekaku off and calling him a public nuisance, the man hit him on the head several times with a broom and knocked him out. At the moment he regained consciousness, Ekaku suddenly penetrated his koan to the depths. Laughing aloud and clapping and dancing with joy along the dusty village streets, he soon attracted the attention of onlookers. Convinced that the poor monk had been knocked silly, they made a large berth around him, yelling, "A madman, a madman! Get out of his way!"

When Ekaku returned to the hermitage, Dokyo immediately recognized the change in his disciple. After a few testing questions, he gave him his approval and a hearty pat on the back. Then, admonishing him to give up his austere practices and to restore himself to health, Dokyo recommended he see the famed Taoist healer Hakuyu in his mountain cave on the outskirts of Kyoto.

Part sage and part madman, Hakuyu was the subject of extraordinary rumors and village tales of a "two-hundred-year-old mountain deity" equipped with supernatural powers. Ekaku, a true believer in village folklore, set out immediately to find the miracle worker. In his most famous book *Yasen kanna (Chat on a Boat in the Evening)*, Hakuin later gave a detailed description of his encounter with the hermit who eventually cured him of his "Zen sickness."

Diagnosing the monk's pitiable condition to be the result of strenuous meditation practice, Hakuyu introduced him to the practice of *naikan*, a mental imagery technique designed to induce healing. First he had Ekaku concentrate his breath energy on the *hara*, a point two inches below the navel. Soon Ekaku experienced a feeling of warmth that enshrouded his entire body and inured him to the biting January cold. He scrupulously followed Hakuyu's wholesome diet and regimen of physical and mental exercises, which included visualizing an exquisitely colored, fragrant lump of cream on his head slowly melting and gradually filtering down throughout his entire body. The delicious fragrance, combined with a feeling of gentle prickling and warmth, would, according to Hakuyu, clear away adhesions and obstructions, tranquilize the organs, and restore a degree of health "far surpassing one's condition at the peak of youth."

Ekaku practiced *naikan* every day for three years, during which all his physical and mental maladies disappeared. *Naikan* changed Ekaku's Zen practice, too; he became less extreme and more balanced. Working alone on various koans, especially on the difficult "Five Ranks of Master Tozan Ryokai," he experienced several *kensho* within only a few months, sometimes breaking into loud, joyous laughter and rolling on the ground in rapture. Again passersby took him for a madman, and soon stories about the "crazy itinerant monk" began to spread. Ekaku enjoyed roaming about in the country as a "madman," but that did not keep him from interrupting his travels for several months to deepen his practice and test his understanding with the various Zen masters of the temples he visited en route. Finally, in the winter of 1715, he built himself a little hermitage close to the village of Yamanoue, where Kanzan Zenji, the founder of the famous monastery Myoshinji in Kyoto, had spent several years in seclusion.

Two years later Ekaku's idyllic life came to an abrupt end when a servant from his home village of Hara arrived at his hut and reported that Ekaku's father was gravely ill. To fulfill his father's last wish to see him, Ekaku returned to Hara—only to find that his father had died. Hoping to visit his ordination temple, Shoinji, Ekaku was further dismayed to find it without an abbot and in a state of near collapse. Once a beautiful little temple, Shoinji was now nothing more than a roofless, floorless ruin. Ekaku had to wear a rain hat and high-heeled wooden sandals to avoid being soaked by rainfall and enormous puddles in what had once been the main hall. All the temple property was in the hands of creditors, and its priestly belongings were mortgaged to merchants. Undaunted, Ekaku decided then and there that he would move in and become the master of Shoinji. Filled with optimism, he performed the "ceremony of entering the monastery" alone in the empty ruin and installed himself as abbot on the spot. Here he would spend the rest of his life. In celebration of this event, Ekaku gave himself a new Dharma name—Hakuin—Hidden in the Whiteness. In Buddhism, whiteness symbolizes essential nature, the place beyond life and death where all suffering has ceased. It is said that when Shakyamuni Buddha died, two blooming sala trees grieved so deeply that they withered and turned white. Alluding to this "white" place of original innocence and purity, the new abbot of Shoinji would sign all his letters and documents, "Hakuin, the old heretic who sits under the sala tree."

Not long after Hakuin arrived at Shoinji, he was honored with an invitation to become *shuso*, the head monk of a *kessei* at Myoshinji in Kyoto. Most Japanese monks would have used this excellent opportunity to establish themselves at Myoshinji, the country's most famous Rinzai monastery; it represented the almost sure path to becoming an "old teacher," a *roshi*. Not Hakuin. He reluctantly accepted the temporary post and returned to Shoinji as soon as the three-month period ended, rejecting an offer to stay on and become a training master.

Hakuin was soon joined by a young disaffected Myoshinji novice. Others followed, and within a short time—to the outrage of the religious establishment—Hakuin had collected as disciples a mixed bag of monks and nuns, and laymen and laywomen. A spiritually gifted sixteen-year-old girl named Satsu was among the first to join what Hakuin called his Thornbush Thicket Community, an ironic response to accusations that he was "entangling people in delusion." Hakuin was a dedicated teacher, available to his little community daily for almost twenty years, though Shoinji boasted only eight resident monks and a few temporary laypersons. Throughout his tenure, Hakuin himself continued to have major experiences of insight. Like one of his great idols, the Chinese Sung dynasty Zen master Daie Soko (Ta-hui Tsung-Kao), he claimed to have experienced eighteen great *satori* and countless "small" openings *(kensho)* throughout his lifetime.

By 1740, with Hakuin now middle-aged and gaining a reputation beyond Hara, the community expanded, adding new buildings for practice and residence. Hakuin still insisted on teaching lay students, but now only monks were allowed to take up residence in the monastery. Here, his colorful diatribes against the Pure Land School of Buddhism and the "silent illumination Zen" of various Soto and Rinzai teachers especially attracted eager young monks. These inexperienced novices were greatly moved by Hakuin's insistence that they cultivate "heroic determination" on the path to enlightenment. Harkening to his example, they, too, were willing to face painful trials as they fashioned themselves into a new generation of Japanese Rinzai Zen monks.

The success of Hakuin's lectures resulted in many invitations to give Dharma talks at various other Zen temples, and even at feudal castles. This boosted his innate self-confidence even further, as reflected in contemporary writings describing Hakuin as an "extraordinary figure," "glaring at people like a tiger," and "walking like a bull." During this period, he rediscovered the artistic talents of his youth and again started to paint and write, leaving several important literary works to be published by his students after his death. The *Orategama (Kettle of No Presence)* is a collection of letters to various Zen practitioners; the *Yabukoji (Evergreen Shrub)* is a letter to the lord of Okayama castle on the practice of Zen; and the *Hebiichigo (Snake-Strawberry)* is a letter to a feudal lord laying out the rules for the virtuous ruler, including cautions directed at tyrannical officials. Hakuin delighted in painting his favorite Zen masters, eccentric wanderers like Ikkyu and Daito; his self-portraits and sketches of animals and folk deities are hilariously funny and show the comic side of the "fierce bull." Hakuin often added verses to his various self-portraits that reflect his joy in violent language.

> In the realm of the thousand Buddhas
> He is hated by the thousand Buddhas
> Among the crowd of demons
> He is detested by the crowd of demons.
> He crushes the silent-illumination heretics of today,
> And massacres the heterodox blind monks of this
>   generation.
> This filthy blind old bald-headed heretic
> Adds more foulness still to foulness.

At the age of sixty, Hakuin's creative output reached its spiritual apex in his invention of the koan, "The Sound of the Single Hand." This act alone has given him a place among the great masters of Zen Buddhism. In a letter to a feudal lord he describes the effects of the use of this koan.

> I made up my mind to instruct everyone by saying, "Listen to the Sound of the Single Hand." I have come to realize that this koan is infinitely more effective in instructing people than any of the methods I had used before. It seems to raise the ball of doubt in people much more easily and the readiness with which progress is made has been as different as the clouds are from the earth. Thus I have come to encourage the meditation on the Single Hand exclusively.

Rumors of the success of this new koan soon began to spread; attracted by the master's fame, hundreds of monks from all over Japan flocked to Hakuin's temple. The three-month training periods at Shoinji now resembled the famous mass audience preachings of Bankei. Lecture demands became more frequent, and Hakuin had to travel for months in order to fulfill his teaching obligations. More and more he began to stress the importance of "passing on the Dharma" to an able successor who would maintain the teaching and attract many students.

In 1749 he found such a person in Torei Enji, a twenty-nine-year-old monk with extraordinary teaching ability. Making him his first Dharma successor in 1760, Hakuin installed Torei as abbot of the newly renovated Ryutakuji temple near the little town of Mishima. Two hundred years later, this monastery, under its famous abbot Nakagawa Soen Roshi, would become the training ground for contemporary Western Zen masters like Robert Aitken and Philip Kapleau. Though his influence was to spread far beyond Japan, Hakuin did not meet the student who was to directly carry on his lineage until three years before his death. Gasan Jito, a brilliant young monk who had received transmission from Rinzai master Gessen Zen'e, decided to investigate Hakuin's teaching. Like the young Ekaku, Gasan was supremely confident that the "old monk" had nothing to teach him that he didn't already know. Three times he entered Hakuin's chamber to show his realization, and three times he was driven out by the old master. Conceding his defeat, Gasan later remarked, "This great priest of the nation struck me three times with his fierce hands and legs and put me on the spot." After Hakuin's death, having finally received formal transmission from the old master, Gasan moved to Rinsho-in, a temple in Edo, where he attracted more than five hundred disciples. He, in turn, produced two innovative successors, Inzan Ien and Takuju Kosen, who together would put the raw koan system that they inherited from Hakuin and Gasan into its final form, creating an ingeniously wrought device for deepening Zen insight after the initial realization experience.

Hakuin, who kept up his remarkably good health into his late seventies, spent his last three years often ill and unable to teach. But his iron will kept him going, nourishing his calligraphy and painting, whose simplified, flat, and liberated brush strokes came to represent the acme of Zen art. Feeling his life ebbing, he tried to spend as much time as possible with his students, still holding to the passionate teaching style that had characterized his entire career. Three days before his death, he put one of his eleven main Dharma successors in charge of all monastery affairs and, on 10

December 1768, at the age of eighty-three, died peacefully in his sleep. Hakuin did not leave a traditional death poem, but he left Japanese Rinzai Zen invigorated and reformed, ready to continue for generations to come.

Hakuin's teaching can be divided into two major parts that to this very day form the core of Japanese Rinzai Zen.

1. Zen students must develop the Great Doubt through uninterrupted meditation practice on an ultimate question (koan). After a certain period of time this Great Doubt will be split open by an experience of Great Death, in which the essential nature of all things is realized. The ensuing intense feeling of Great Joy opens up a well of love and compassion and provides the necessary incentive to continuously deepen one's Zen practice.

2. Having achieved a glimpse of the undivided fundamental reality, it becomes the task of the Zen student to apply this experience in the differentiated world of the myriad things; morality and practice blend in such a way that the direct application of one's experience is the action of love and compassion toward all beings. "I" and "others," though on the phenomenal level clearly distinct, are understood as fundamentally identical. Without morality there can be no true practice. Thus, the myth of the "enlightened" Zen master whose actions are beyond the level of good and evil is destroyed. Since the body is the vehicle for enlightenment, it is important to preserve it carefully. Hakuin painfully realized that merciless treatment of the body in order to achieve a mystic breakthrough could end in premature death and thereby accomplish nothing.

It is important to examine in detail these two pillars of Hakuin's teaching in order to find out how they connect with daily life.

Hakuin recognized that the pattern of Great Doubt, Great Death, and Great Joy was the fundamental process of any valid religious experience. In order to get this process started, it was first necessary to evoke the Great Doubt. According to him, it was the task of a genuine teacher to do that with the help of a beginner koan, preferably "Joshu's Mu" or "The Sound of the Single Hand." These koans served as mental devices designed to break the habitual pattern of sequential thought with its never-ending cycle of concepts and mental images. Using parts of Hakuyu's *naikan* practice, Hakuin advised his students to connect their koan-focused consciousness with the area below the navel. "If this settled concentration power can be maintained for several hours," he counseled, "the student will advance determinedly and the Great Doubt will appear." The important thing was to discard all emotions, concepts, and thoughts by maintaining single-minded concentration on one koan-thought. Hakuin maintained that it was not always absolutely necessary to sit in meditation in a quiet place, but that it was essential to carry the koan about in one's consciousness in all situations—active or static, noisy or quiet. This state of nonconceptual awareness, often compared to a "field of ice" or a "dry desert where nothing grows," is what he referred to as the Great Doubt. And he used all kinds of devices to prod his students into this promising condition. Sometimes he would inspire them with fantastic stories about Zen students of earlier times who had sat completely motionless in the middle of a swamp surrounded by millions of bloodthirsty mosquitoes; or he would repeat his teacher Dokyo's story about sitting all night in an abandoned graveyard, oblivious to a pack of hungry, circling wolves. Although intended to free the student's latent *joriki*, or concentration power, Hakuin's stories were never quite free of exaggeration borne of his own fascination with the "determined warrior." Aroused by such stories, and often moved to tears, several of his disciples took his advice too literally. The graves of these young Zen monks at Shoinji cemetery bear witness to this major weakness in Hakuin's personality.

The transition from the Great Doubt to the Great Death is beyond description, and, according to Hakuin, a matter of "sudden transformation beyond one's will." Often a small perception, like the sound of a bell, the smell of incense, or a feeling of physical pain could trigger this experience of seeing into one's own nature. In this context, he described the "absolute certainty of a knowledge of Truth" that occurs at that moment. Later reflections or rational explanations of the experience could only end in error and the stale feeling of "talking about something." But out of the immediacy of being confirmed by the temple bell or the fragrance of incense arises the wave of Great Joy, the feeling that everything is all right from the very beginning, or, to put it in Hakuin's own words: "There is no enlightenment one must seek."

For Hakuin, koan practice was the absolute focal point of Zen training. He saw it as the only method by which a student could be brought to genuine insight, and he never tired of railing against the "silent illumination" practice of other Zen masters, particularly those of the Soto sect. Zen without strict koan practice was a perversion of the "true teachings of the ancients," and much worse, the waste of a human being's life, a birth "so difficult to attain." Pulling out all the oratorical stops, Hakuin admonished his students against even thinking about such practices.

There are some blind, bald idiots who stand in a calm, unper-
turbed, untouchable place and consider that the state of
mind produced in this atmosphere comprises seeing into
their own natures. They think that to polish and perfect
purity is sufficient, but have never even in a dream achieved
the state of enlightenment. People of this sort spend all day
practicing non-action and end up by having practiced action
all the while; they spend all day practicing non-creating and
end up by having practiced creating all the while. Why is
this so? It is because their insight into the Way is not clear,
because they can't arrive at the truth of the Dharma-nature.

He had equally harsh words for practitioners of the Pure Land
School of Buddhism who believed in a paradise distinct from
this world, and a mythical intermediary called Amida Buddha,
without whose help no salvation was possible. "Outside your
own mind there is no Pure Land; outside your own body, there
is no buddha," Hakuin preached, adding that all "true ancestors"
of the Zen tradition "never once, even inadvertently, spoke of a
rebirth in the Pure Land." He taught that only with the experience of seeing into one's own nature—effected by genuine koan
practice—could one see that "this body is the buddha from the
very beginning." He deplored Zen masters who tried to incorporate Pure Land elements into the technique of sitting meditation, and warned:

Some two hundred years ago evil and careless Zen followers decimated the Zen monasteries and corrupted the true
style of Zen, spreading the vulgar and debased heretical
understanding of the Pure Land School.... If Zen is com-

bined with Pure Land, it cannot last for long and will surely be destroyed.

To those Pure Land followers who would listen, he suggested altering their practice in such a way that calling the buddha's name or reciting the first line of the *Lotus Sutra* would become more like concentrating on a koan without any expectation of being "saved from outside." Remembering his mother's devotion to the Nichiren school, Hakuin set up a detailed course of meditation for Nichiren followers, which of course turned out to be nothing but a variation on the theme of koan practice.

The practice of the Lotus Sutra is from today on to determine, despite happiness and pain, sadness and joy, whether asleep or awake, standing or reclining, to intone without interruption the title of the sutra alone: *Namu Myoho renge kyo*. Whether you use this title as a staff or as a source of strength, you must recite it with the fervent desire to see without fail the True Face of the Lotus. Make each inhalation and exhalation of your breath the title of the sutra…. Then you will awaken to the Great Matter of true meditation….You will see right before you, in the place where you stand, the True Face of the Lotus, and at once your body and mind will drop off.

Hakuin was unsuccessful at converting Pure Land and Nichiren Buddhism into Zen. But that did not stop him from preaching his views widely and forcefully. To the last, he never changed his mind on this subject.

Although he himself passed only a few koans with his teacher Dokyo Etan and never bothered to finish his koan practice with him, Hakuin went on to create a koan curriculum that eventually replaced all previous methods of Zen instruction. What has come to be known as Hakuin Zen is the final product of his work, refined by Gasan Jito, Inzan Ien, and Takuju Kosen. Hakuin's koan system demands that after a *kensho* experience with the initial koan "Mu" or "The Sound of the Single Hand," the student must progress through a specified series of koans compiled in old Chinese collections like *The Blue Cliff Record*, *The Gateless Gate*, or *The Record of Rinzai*. The koans vary in order and type, and the student engages in a long and intensive process of clarifying the essential points of up to five hundred of them. Using a fivefold classification system, Hakuin and his Dharma heirs systematized and categorized the most important koans.

Hosshin koans* are intended to deepen initial insight into the undifferentiated realm of *shunyata* (emptiness, or suchness). One of the most famous of these is the verse of the sixth-century Chinese Zen master Fu Daishi (Shan Hui).

> With hands of emptiness I take hold of the plow;
> While walking, I ride the water buffalo.

Kikan koans lead the Zen student to a better understanding of the differentiated, phenomenal world as seen with the "enlightened eye." These koans are extremely important in helping the student to avoid "Zen sickness," or getting stuck in the realm of emptiness and being robbed of the energy to deal with the distinctly differentiated level of reality. Case 37 in *The Gateless Gate* is such a koan.

---

* We are indebted to Isshu Miura and Ruth Fuller Sasaki for their explanation of Hakuin's koan system in Zen Dust (New York: Harcourt, Brace, and World, 1966), now unfortunately out of print.

> A monk asked Joshu, "What is the meaning of Bodhi-
> dharma coming from the West?"
> Joshu said, "Oaktree in the garden."

Another example is the "Three Barriers" koan of the Sung
dynasty master Tosotsu Juetsu (Tou-shuai Ts'ung-yueh), devised
to test the Zen understanding of his students.

> The purpose of going to abandoned, grassy places and doing
> zazen is to search for our self-nature. Now, at this moment,
> where is your self-nature?
>
> When you have attained your self-nature, you can free
> yourself from birth and death. How would you free yourself
> when you are about to die?
>
> When you have freed yourself from birth and death, you
> will know where to go. After your death, where do you go?

Of course, these barriers correspond to the perennial questions
of humankind: "Who am I? Where do I come from? Where will
I go?" Generally, these questions are considered to be unanswer-
able, but for the Zen student who has had a true realization experience, they can be answered on the spot.

Gonsen koans help the student to clarify the difficult words and
phrases of Zen ancestors. These exchanges open up a hidden
world of beauty and wisdom, which, once penetrated, is as clear
as the song of the thrush.

> A monk asked the priest Fuketsu (Feng-hsueh Yen-chao),
> "Speech and silence are concerned with subject and object.
> How can I transcend both subject and object?"

Fuketsu said, "I always think of Konan [a province in China] in March. Partridges chirp among the many fragrant blossoms."

Another famous example of a *gonsen* koan is the "Three Turning Words" of the early Sung Zen master Haryo Kokan (Pa Ling).

A monk asked Haryo, "What is the Deva sect?"
Haryo said, "Snow in a silver bowl."
"What is the Tao?"
"The clearly enlightened man falls into a well."
"What is the sharpest sword?"
"The dew on the top of each branch of coral reflects the light of the moon."

Nanto koans are difficult to pass through, since they point to a subtle place beyond right and wrong, where, in the midst of daily activity, the Zen student can develop composure and peace of mind. Hakuin advised his students to "quickly settle these *nanto* koans once and for all," since the tranquillity of mind that followed was, for him, the sure sign of the confident Zen person. He felt that Case 38 in *The Gateless Gate* was an excellent example of an especially difficult *nanto* koan.

The priest Goso (Wu-tsu Fa-yen) said, "It is like a water buffalo passing through a window. Its head, horns, and four legs all pass through. Why can't its tail pass through too?"

The last group, the highly valued *goi* koans, were, according to Hakuin, "spiritual jewels," for they had triggered several enlightenment experiences in the great master himself. These koans are associated with the "Five Ranks of Master Tozan Ryokai," a T'ang Zen master who had composed verses on the "five modes of the apparent and the real." Hakuin wrote a lengthy commentary on these verses, lauding them as "the ship that carries the Zen student across the poisonous sea."

Still he felt it necessary to add one more step after the completion of the *goi* koans that formally ended his program. Espousing moral conduct in daily life as the practical cornerstone of his teaching, Hakuin had his students go over the Ten Buddhist Precepts. He urged them to be guided by their ethical spirit in applying Zen to their lives, for the precepts were indeed the ultimate aim of Zen practice. And he further insisted that the practice never really reached an end, but rather progressed and deepened throughout one's life. The Ten Buddhist Precepts, which are not killing, not stealing, not misusing sex, not lying, not giving or taking drugs, not discussing faults of others, not praising yourself while abusing others, not sparing the Dharma assets, not indulging in anger, and not defaming the Buddha, Dharma, and Sangha, are guidelines rather than commandments etched in stone. Following the way of the bodhisattva ideal, they point the ethically motivated Buddhist toward the ultimate goal of saving all beings.

Though renowned for his rough manners and crude speech, Hakuin was motivated by a strong ethical sense throughout his life. He was committed to the commonfolk, often interceding on their behalf with their samurai overlords in a plea for compassion and social justice. He openly enjoined feudal lords to prove their spiritual attainment by proving in word and deed that as "enlightened rulers" they had the well-being of their subjects in mind. On his various lecture tours, he would often stop in small villages and deliver free talks to laypeople, always finding simple words to convey his teaching. Hakuin had the remarkable gift of adapting his style and language to his audience. He always spoke extemporaneously, using the power and spontaneity of the moment to get his point across.

But Hakuin could never escape his samurai heritage; his fascination with the "strong warrior" led him to elevate the samurai class, even to the extent of praising the strength and "wisdom" of the cruel shogun Ieyasu, founder of the Tokugawa clan. Using the samurai preoccupation with death as a teaching tool, he advised feudal lords and high-status retainers to investigate the word *shi*, "death," in the same way that he assigned to his monks the koan "Mu." Once the warrior had escaped the realm of life and death in the experience of *satori*, he could reemerge as a brave and moral fighter, loyal to his lord and compassionate toward the common people. Such reasoning led Hakuin to exalt the contemporary *bushido* code.

A warrior must from the beginning to the end be physically strong. In his attendance on his duties and in his relationships with others the most rigid punctiliousness and propriety are required. His hair must be properly dressed, his garments in the strictest order, and his swords must be fastened at his side. With this exact and proper deportment, the true meditation stands forth with an overflowing splendor. Mounted on a sturdy horse, the warrior can ride forth to face an uncountable horde of enemies as though he were riding into a place empty of people. The valiant undaunted expression on his face reflects his practice of the peerless, true, uninterrupted meditation sitting. Meditating in this way, the warrior can accomplish in one month what it takes the monk a year to do; in three days he can open up for himself benefits that would take the monk a hundred days.

On another occasion, however, he could just as fervently admonish a feudal lord, urging him to give up his riches, "clean up the garden, change the water in the basins, and with a laughing face wash the feet of a retainer's horse." He could also vent his public contempt for power-hungry "idiotic" generals who didn't care about the welfare of the common people. Cautioning "tyrannical officials" who plundered the citizenry and made them suffer, Hakuin wrote: "When the common people decline, the nation will surely perish." Only the benevolent lord "whose heart is deeply motivated by compassion" had a natural right to rule.

In a nation where a woman's status was often less than that of a horse or a cow, Hakuin pleaded with feudal lords to alter the situation, claiming that "women, after all, are human beings" deserving of the "greatest respect and dignity." His own conduct toward women was quite in advance of his time. Among his lay students there were several with whom he enjoyed lively Zen exchanges characterized by a standard of absolute equality. One famous anecdote involves an elderly Hara woman who had heard Hakuin say in a lecture, "Mind is the Pure Land, the body itself is Amida Buddha." Pondering this for days, the old woman had a *kensho* experience one morning while washing a pot. She immediately rushed over to Shoinji and appeared before Hakuin, crying "Amida Buddha has crashed into my body. Mountains and rivers shine wonderfully. How marvelous!"

"What's that?" Hakuin snorted. "Nothing can shine in your asshole!"

Pushing him aside and jumping with joy, the old woman cried out, "Hakuin is not enlightened yet!"

Hearing this, Hakuin clapped her on the back and roared with laughter.

The sixteen-year-old Satsu, who frequently saw Hakuin in private interviews *(dokusan)*, loved to tease the old master. One day he explained to her a difficult passage in a sutra and asked, "Do you understand?"

She responded, "Please, could you explain it again?" Then, just as he was about to open his mouth, she got up and left the room, leaving behind a laughing Hakuin.

"I've been made a fool by this girl!" he shouted after her.

Hakuin's humor is especially evident in the many paintings he left behind. Always poking fun at people, he indulged in caricatures and often accompanied them with funny verses. He also loved to make fun of himself, and delighted in comparing his own tumbledown Shoinji to rich Kyoto temples like Daitokuji and Myoshinji. Like his great idol, the Muromachi master Ikkyu, he railed against the "establishment priests" who had lost touch with the true way of the *unsui*, the "drifting cloud."

Often Zen masters, and their students as well, make constant abundance into luxurious living, and the prosperity of the temple gives the style to the teaching. They think that eloquence and a clever tongue make for wisdom, equate fine food and clothing with the Buddha Way, make haughtiness and beauty into moral qualities, and take the faith exhibited by others as an indication that they themselves have attained the Dharma…. They adorn themselves lavishly in silken gowns and preach recklessly…. In deftly acquiring offerings of money that represent much backbreaking toil on the part of the populace, they would appear to have gained miraculous powers.... But when the time to die arrives and the solitary lamp flickers as they lie halfway between life and death, they cry and moan. Driven mad, with no place to put their hands and feet, they die so agonizing a death that their disciples and followers cannot bear to look at them.

Hakuin enjoyed indulging in humorous folktales and often used them to teach common people the importance of basic ethics. His superstitious belief in the supernatural powers of certain Buddhist sutras stands in contrast to his strict adherence to koan practice and his tirades against the dualism of Pure Land followers. But his interaction with the Taoist hermit and healer Hakuyu, and the success of the latter's *naikan* therapy, had convinced him of the existence of certain "inexplicable powers," which, as long as they did not conflict with his Zen practice, should be taken seriously.

Hakuin was a gifted artist; his paintings and calligraphy, as well as his voluminous writings, reflect a universally talented personality. Following the tradition of Japanese ink painting known as *suiboku-ga*, he developed his own dynamic Zen style and carried it beyond the traditional boundaries. In his inimitable, eccentric way, he depicted humane and earthy subjects, executed in light shades of black ink, exchanging formal aesthetic values for an appreciation of the coarse and ugly. To the joy of lower-class people who loved his rude humor, Hakuin expressed his own idiosyncratic views in his rough paintings. Using animals to convey human characteristics, he poked fun at conventionalized Tokugawa notions of morality.

All current Japanese Rinzai Zen masters trace their lineage back to Hakuin Ekaku Zenji. It was his merit to develop the raw concept of the famous Chinese Zen master Daie Soko (1089–1163), who had emphasized the importance of continued practice after the initial awakening. Hakuin single-handedly created a koan system that has helped generations of Zen practitioners to realize their own nature. It was he, too, who strongly emphasized the need for Dharma successors who would transmit "true Zen practice" to future generations. According to Hakuin, a Zen master must be completely devoted to teaching Zen, but he must never believe that he has "completed" his own practice, for moral refinement, combined with ever deeper experiences of insight, continues forever.

The last six lines of his "Zazen Wasan" ("A Song in Praise of Sitting Meditation"), a short religious poem that is recited to this very day in every Japanese Rinzai Zen monastery, expresses the essence of "Hakuin Zen."

> Boundless and free is the sky of *samadhi* [absorption],
> Bright the full moon of wisdom!
> Truly, is anything missing now?
> Nirvana is right here, before our eyes;
> This very place is the Lotus Land,
> This very body, the Buddha.

7

Nyogen Senzaki:
The Homeless Mushroom

N yogen Senzaki was born in 1876, a year before the end of the era of the samurai in Japan. This momentous break with the past played itself out in the life of this homeless wandering monk, who single-handedly brought a modern form of democratized Zen to the West. Nyogen Senzaki's path, like the revolutionary events that characterized the Meiji era in which he developed his radical principles, was difficult and fraught with obstacles. It is essential to take a close look at the society that formed him.

The Meiji regime prohibited all samurai from bearing swords, the symbol of their superior status. In addition, the warrior caste lost its stipends, which were compulsorily converted into government bonds representing only about half their value. In a desperate last attempt to turn back the clock, Saigo Takamori, a samurai endowed with the virtues of his birth—courage, generosity, lack of ostentation, and contempt for money—organized a rebellion to overthrow the eight-year rule of Emperor Meiji. This "civil war of Seinan" ended in 1877 with the devastating defeat of Takamori's forces. The proud rebel samurai leader was forced to commit *seppuku*, leaving a triumphant new regime in place of a two-hundred-sixty-year order that had outlived its usefulness.

The beginnings of the Meiji restoration are traced to the appearance of four American "black ships," led by Commander Matthew Perry, offshore of the Japanese town of Uraga in the summer of 1853. Threatening the Tokugawa regime with attack, Perry eventually forced the opening of two Japanese ports to American trade ships, thus ending more than two hundred years of self-imposed isolation. Soon other powers like Great Britain, Russia, France, and Germany followed, and within five years, treaties for the further opening of Japan to foreign trade were put into effect. These events, and their ineffectual handling by the Tokugawa regime, convinced the Japanese that the weak Bakufu government was ready to be done away with. In 1860, a group of nationalistic samurai assassinated the powerful regent Ii Naosuke, who ruled for the minor shogun Iemochi Tokugawa, thus opening the way for a series of challenges to Tokugawa rule that were to become steadily more effective with the years.

Between 1860 and 1867, the Bakufu tried desperately to regain its old strength, implementing policies designed to give the government control of all trade. In May 1860, a decree was issued granting monopoly rights in the major export consignments of grains, raw silk, and wax to certain Edo wholesalers. All shipments had to depart from Yokohama, Edo's port, ensuring the Bakufu's control over principal items of export. However, the government did not have the power to enforce the decree in the domains of the increasingly powerful *daimyo*, the feudal lords, and finally, in 1864, the monopoly was abolished, leaving trade to develop according to the free market.

At the same time, jingoistic lower-class samurai murdered several British and American trade officials, provoking Western retaliation. In 1863, the lords of two southern domains, Choshu and Satsuma, decided to start their own private war against the hated *gaijin*. Choshu steamers attacked American, French, and Dutch vessels in the Shimonoseki Straits. Satsuma forces attacked a British squadron near Kagoshima, inflicting heavy damage on the British ships. The allied forces of France, Britain, and the United States retaliated, bombarding Shimonoseki, and forcing Choshu and Satsuma to a truce and the Tokugawa regime to the payment of an indemnity. The irrational, antiforeign sentiment of the Japanese ruling elite was cooled by these belligerent events, and they were forced to make peace with foreign infiltration of the country.

Their defeat had taught the lords of the Satsuma, Choshu, Nagato, and Hizen districts another lesson too: since the Bakufu was too weak to punish their rebellious districts for engaging in independent warfare against the Western powers, it would probably be too weak to withstand a united action to establish a new regime under the flag of the young emperor Meiji. On the morning of January 3, 1868, troops under the leadership of Satsuma seized the imperial palace in Kyoto. A council was summoned, the last shogun Yoshinobu Tokugawa was stripped of his lands and power, and Emperor Meiji was formally restored to political leadership. Almost three centuries of Tokugawa rule thus ended, and a new era, the Meiji restoration, began.

Twenty-five years later, the new regime had completely changed Japanese society, making the empire a world power equal to its European counterparts. The architects of the Meiji regime were a small elite of relatively young men, a mixture of lower-class samurai and court nobility. In the so-called Charter Oath, the regime, in the name of the young emperor, adopted new principles as guidelines for the nation. Old Tokugawa rules regulating in detail the activities of men and women were abolished, and all classes were urged to unite in an effort to establish a modern nation-state, which included opening Japan to Western technology and culture. The new government initiated a Westernized educational system, postal service, military conscription, telegraph, railroads, and finally, in 1889, a constitution and a national assembly, the Diet. Meiji government officials studied various European and American societies, taking from each what they thought would best fit Japan. They based the legal system on the French Napoleonic Code, the education system on American pragmatism, and the constitution on its authoritarian German twin. Most importantly, the old feudal system was abolished, and the division of the country into prefectures turned powerful *daimyo* into local governors, responsible for keeping law and order in the name of the emperor.

The city of Edo was renamed Tokyo and designated the imperial capital. The new spirit of "modernity" infused the automation of agriculture and the development of industry. In order to fulfill its dream of turning Japan into a first-class, modern nation state as quickly as possible, the government supported "corporate capitalism," placing economic power in the hands of *zaibatsu*, an exclusive clique of private entrepreneurs who enjoyed a virtual monopoly in finance, industry, and commerce, in close cooperation with the military and the imperial court. The new Japanese capitalism, characterized by a predominant state enterprise supported by a financial oligarchy, heavily taxed the population, particularly the agricultural community.

Following the ancient Japanese model of *saisei-itchi*, the unity of religion and government, the Meiji regime created State Shinto, a mixture of emperor worship, obedience to state authorities, and the worship of *kami*, various Shinto nature gods that were thought to protect the "superiority" of Japanese society. Rather than relegating religious matters to temple authorities, the government itself controlled the activities of State Shinto, gearing it carefully toward ethnocentric nationalism. In this vein, deifying the emperor as a "living *kami*" was a clever move on the part of powerful bureaucrats and militaristic nationalists, who used the exaltation of the throne to promote nationalistic fervor among the masses. Far from directing affairs of state, the emperor was no more than a convenient figurehead for a small despotic oligarchy. In an attempt to spread State Shinto, the government moved to weaken Buddhism by instigating anti-Buddhist propaganda that linked Buddhism to the hated Tokugawa regime. As a result, many Buddhist temples were destroyed or damaged, a large number of monks and nuns were forced to take up secular life, and all Buddhist priests were encouraged to marry.

Forced to conduct Shinto ceremonies, Buddhist clergy tried to save their religion by aligning themselves with the nationalistic sentiment of the Meiji regime. In addition, both Shintoism and Buddhism attacked the newly legalized Christian religion on grounds that a doctrine of love and forgiveness was "inherently antinationalistic and un-Japanese."

By the early 1890s, the Meiji government felt strong enough to compete with the Western powers in their imperialistic advances aimed at exploiting China. Using disputes over Chinese influence in Korea as a pretense, Japan declared war on China in the summer of 1894, and soon controlled Korea and the southern part of Manchuria. In February 1895, Japanese forces took the Liaotung peninsula, including Port Arthur, forcing China to accept defeat and a harsh peace treaty. China lost Taiwan to Japan, but with the help of the "triple intervention" powers of Germany, France, and Russia, the Meiji government was forced to return the Liaotung peninsula. But only five years later, Japan helped Great Britain subdue the Chinese Boxer rebellion, and was rewarded by the government in London with an alliance treaty. Now backed by Britain, Japan felt strong enough to attack expansionist Russian forces that had crossed the frontier into Korea. Within one year, the Japanese inflicted major defeats on the Russian army and navy at Port Arthur and Tsushima. Plagued by internal problems, Russia was forced to sign a peace treaty in 1905, ceding to Japan its holdings in southern Manchuria, the southern half of the island of Sakhalin, and the Liaotung peninsula.

Japan's military success propelled the nation to world power status, which manifested itself in a jingoistic frenzy that forced the half-Russian, half-Japanese pacifist monk Nyogen Senzaki to leave his country and start a new life in the United States. Indelibly marked on his mind were the pernicious effects of nationalism, and the opportunism of the Buddhist establishment in the face of state power.

The circumstances of Nyogen's birth and early childhood are not well known and with the course of time have taken on an apocryphal character. Born to a Japanese mother in October 1876, on the Siberian peninsula of Kamchatka, he was either abandoned by her at birth, or left to survive after she died in childbirth. His father remains unknown, but it is generally assumed that he was either Russian or Chinese. A traveling Japanese Kegon Buddhist priest decided to adopt the baby and take it to Japan.

Nyogen was given a first-class education. At the age of five, he was already studying the Chinese classics, and before the age of eighteen, he had finished reading the multi-volume Chinese Tripitaka, the Buddhist "Bible." Drawn to medicine, Nyogen was looking forward to starting medical school, when suddenly his foster father passed away. The death of his only family member left deep scars on the psyche of the eighteen-year-old youth. He resolved on the spot to renounce the secular life and devote himself, like his foster father, to religious and moral teaching. Nyogen was ordained by a Shingon priest, but, soon disappointed by the institutionalized formality of esoteric Buddhism, he left Shingon for Zen. A Soto priest accepted the young novice, but Nyogen wandered away again, this time turning up at the gates of the Rinzai monastery Engakuji in Kamakura. Impressed by his previous correspondence with its young abbot Soyen Shaku, the twenty-year-old Nyogen resolved to stick with Rinzai Zen in the hope of catching a glimpse of his essential nature.

Abbot Soyen Shaku was the Zen prodigy of the day. Having received transmission at the incredibly young age of twenty-five from Kosen Roshi, the most celebrated Zen master of his time, Soyen was sent for a year to Keio University in Tokyo to study Buddhism. Stimulated by his new intellectual activity, Soyen decided to spend some time in Southeast Asia studying Theravada Buddhism. Two years after his return to Japan, at the death of his teacher Kosen Roshi, Soyen Shaku was installed as chief abbot of Engakuji at the unprecedented age of thirty-three. In 1893, as the representative of Japanese Zen Buddhism, Soyen Shaku attended the World Parliament of Religions in Chicago, where he made contact with American Buddhists who would invite him back ten years later.

Immediately recognizing the talent of "this strange monk," Soyen drove Nyogen hard, often using the traditionally harsh Rinzai methods of shouting and beating to press his student to self-realization. Nyogen fell ill with tuberculosis, and spent a year in isolation in a little wooden hut on the monastery grounds. Sensing himself to be close to death, Nyogen asked Soyen for his last advice. "If you die, just die," was the cryptic answer of the stern abbot. Strangely enough, Nyogen's health began to improve, and it was not long before he could again engage in the usual demanding monastery schedule. It was during this time that Nyogen met D.T. Suzuki, a young lay student and favorite of Soyen Shaku, who had no idea that he was harboring under his roof the two twentieth-century pioneers of Zen Buddhism in America.

Nyogen's practice progressed, and although he never spoke of his own *kensho* experience, he resolved his first koans during the five years he spent at Engakuji. But here, too, he was discomfited by monastic ceremony and ritual, alienated by the traditional life of a Buddhist priest or monk. Turning to books for intellectual stimulus, Nyogen hit on the writings of the German educational reformer and founder of the kindergarten system, Friedrich Froebel (1782–1852). Froebel's ideas so impressed the young monk that he resolved to leave Engakuji to found a nursery school, which he called the Mentorgarten. Believing in the natural power of children, Nyogen envisioned himself guiding and watching them, and helping them learn about nature without religious instruction or ceremonies. He would later extend this concept of a Mentorgarten to his small Zen centers in San Francisco and Los Angeles.

I coined the word "Mentorgarten" as I thought the whole world was a beautiful garden where all friends could associate peacefully, and be mentors of one another.... As in a kindergarten we had no teacher, but we encouraged one another and tried our best to grow up naturally. And like a nurse of the kindergarten, I sometimes presumed myself as a gardener to do all sorts of labor, but I never forgot that I myself was also a flower of the garden, mingling with old and new friends.... I was always happy in this Mentorgarten, and why will I not be so in the future? This is the…spirit of the Sangha in primitive Buddhism, nay, not only in primitive Buddhism, but in modern Buddhism, so far as it is true Buddhism.

In 1901, after five years at Engakuji, Nyogen asked Soyen Shaku for permission to leave the monastery in order to devote himself to the creation of a kindergarten. Soyen decided to let his "mad monk" go, and gave him a to-whom-it-may-concern letter that read:

Brother Nyogen is a nameless and penniless monk. He goes unrecognized both in and out of monasteries. He has only an aspiration for loving-kindness, with which no honored position can compare. He is bold enough to establish the Mentorgarten with no other assets than his accumulated knowledge of Buddhism and modern thought. To begin with, he will start by taking care of children, trying to influence their parents indirectly. He will plant the seedlings of Buddha in the field of actual life, without depending on the modern church system of Japan.

And that is exactly what Nyogen set out to do. Determined to give children the love and care that he had received from his foster father, he created a kindergarten of about twenty to thirty youngsters. Every morning before opening the playhouse he would sit zazen; he spent the rest of the day with the children, calling their attention to a sunrise or sunset, to differently colored leaves, or to the song of birds.

But in 1905, the increasingly shrill voice of Japanese nationalism left him with no option but to leave. Having been born in Russia, perhaps partly Russian himself, Nyogen looked with relief at the opportunity to accompany Soyen Shaku as his attendant in San Francisco, where the famous abbot had been invited to visit friends and deliver lectures on Buddhism and Zen. America seemed a very promising place for Nyogen Senzaki, who was now almost thirty, and whose distaste for rampant nationalism and institutional religion, what he called "cathedral Zen," prompted him not to return to Japan. Sensing Nyogen's thoughts, Soyen Shaku took him for a walk in Golden Gate Park, and, setting down Nyogen's suitcase, the master said, "Just face the great city and see whether it conquers you or you conquer it. Don't feel obliged to serve me any longer." Disappearing into the evening fog with a goodbye on his lips, Soyen left his student, never to see him again. The master never gave Nyogen formal transmission, and it is not clear whether he gave him permission to teach. It seems that he intended for Nyogen to ripen for at least twenty years until he would be ready to emerge as a Zen teacher in the West. Nyogen had achieved his goal; he would remain in the United States for the rest of his life, returning to his home country only once on a brief trip to visit his friend Nakagawa Soen Roshi in 1955.

Far from being disheartened, Nyogen took on all kinds of jobs to stay alive. He was a houseboy, a cook, elevator operator, clerk, and hotel manager. In 1916 he even managed to buy a hotel, but after only a short period of time he gave it up, feeling very uncomfortable at "playing the boss." When in 1919 he received the message that Soyen Shaku had died in Japan at the age of sixty, Nyogen lit incense and vowed to commemorate his teacher's death every year. From the time of his arrival, he studied English and was a frequent visitor to the San Francisco Public Library, where he spent hours reading authors like Ralph Waldo Emerson and William James. He was especially fond of German culture, often referring to great German philosophers like Immanuel Kant as "true giants," who, like every man, once in a while needed a "good kick in the pants."

In 1922, at the age of forty-six, seventeen years after his arrival in the United States, he spent all his savings to hire a hall and give a lecture on "The First Steps in Meditation." He repeated this procedure several times, and by 1927 had established a "floating zendo," which became popular in San Francisco Buddhist circles. Carrying with him a six-hundred-year-old painting of the bodhisattva Manjushri, who cuts through all delusions, Nyogen established a zendo wherever and whenever he could afford it. He thrived in this atmosphere of impermanence, stressing again and again the importance of "true homelessness" for the unconventional, everyday Zen practitioner. His very name, Nyogen, meaning "like a fantasy," was the perfect synonym for the Zen of a homeless wanderer. With help from his new students and friends, Nyogen was able to rent an apartment on Bush Street, later the location of the first Zen center in the United States. Although he once invited the Japanese roshi Gyodo Furukawa for a brief stay in San Francisco, Nyogen soon realized that the cultural gap between formal Japanese "cathedral Zen," and his own antihierarchical and informal "Mentorgarten Zen" had become too wide ever to be bridged again.

In the early 1930s, Nyogen moved to Los Angeles, celebrating the simple life of a wanderer, with "no excess of food or money, sleeping quietly without worries, and having no possessions." Soon he was able to rent an apartment (in one of the dirtiest parts of town) and slowly acquaint himself with the Japanese community. He continued giving lectures and meditation instruction, living on the dollar bills that his students would leave behind. In 1932, Nyogen met Mrs. Kin Tanahashi, the owner of a small business, who offered him room and board in exchange for care of her mentally retarded son Jimmy. Nyogen, the "mentorgartner," made friends with the twelve-year-old boy, who repaid his kindness by learning the first line of the Four Great Bodhisattva Vows, "Shu jo mu hen sei gan do" ("Though the many beings are numberless, I vow to save them"). These were among the few words Jimmy Tanahashi ever spoke in his short life.

It was Mrs. Tanahashi who directed Nyogen's attention to the poems of the young Japanese Zen monk Nakagawa Soen, which were published in a Japanese language magazine. The two men began a correspondence and resolved to meet each other one day. (See chapter 8 for a description of the meeting between Nyogen Senzaki and Nakagawa Soen Roshi.)

Nyogen spent the greater part of the 1930s establishing his Mentorgarten Meditation Hall. Using simple chairs instead of traditional Japanese *zafus*, he perfectly matched the level of his instructions to his students' ability. Far from resembling an institution, his Mentorgarten provided students with the opportunity to learn the basics of zazen, Mahayana Buddhism, and Japanese art and culture. He patiently delivered lectures every week and invited students to see him privately in informal interviews. Steadily, Nyogen's sangha grew, and with the generous help of Mrs. Tanahashi, he bought appropriate furniture and established a little library.

The year 1942 marked a hiatus in all of Nyogen Senzaki's efforts. The outbreak of World War II and the ensuing anti-Japanese hysteria in the U.S. led to President Roosevelt's Executive Order 9066, mandating the internment of both Japanese aliens and naturalized American citizens. Senzaki and his Japanese community were interned at Heart Mountain Relocation Camp in Wyoming. Now their "Mentorgarten Zen" training paid off; making the best of their situation, they practiced zazen together, chanted Buddhist sutras, and spent many hours listening to Nyogen expound the Buddhadharma. Ruth Strout McCandless, a devoted friend in Los Angeles, took care of Nyogen's library and stayed in touch with the almost seventy-year-old monk, sending him books at his request. The three years in the internment camp gave Nyogen the time and the opportunity to work on lectures; every month he managed to send one back to Los Angeles, where he had entrusted a friend with the administration of the weekly meetings.

Returning to Los Angeles in 1945, Nyogen moved into a small apartment on the top floor of the Miyako hotel. The owner, a fellow-internee, had been so impressed by Nyogen that he gave him the flat rent-free, allowing the old monk to resume his usual Dharma activities. The following thirteen years, until his death at the age of eighty-two, were the most productive in Nyogen's life. Many American students crowded into his room for zazen and a lecture two evenings a week. Among these was Robert Aitken, who appeared in December 1947, and soon became one of Nyogen's most devoted students. Aitken would depart three years later for his first stay as a Zen student in Japan, returning to the States to become one of the first Americans to receive Dharma transmission and the title Roshi.

In these last years of his life, Nyogen touched and enriched the lives of many people who would later disseminate the Dharma in the United States. In 1949, he finally met his long-time correspondent Nakagawa Soen, who was about to be made abbot of Ryutakuji monastery in Mishima, Japan. Nyogen was deeply impressed with Soen and saw in him a likely successor in the West. "Some day the Mentorgarten will disappear," he said to Robert Aitken, "but Soen-san will build a great temple in the United States and the Dharma will flourish." Nyogen's dream was not to be, for Soen's tasks as abbot of a Japanese monastery only allowed him time for frequent visits to the United States, and not, as Nyogen had hoped, permanent residence.

In 1955, at the age of seventy-nine, Nyogen accepted Soen's invitation to visit Japan. Though he spent most of his time at Ryutakuji monastery, he traveled to Kamakura to visit the grave of his beloved teacher Soyen Shaku—from whom he had parted in San Francisco exactly fifty years before. It was a very emotional moment for the old monk, who, true to his vow, had celebrated his teacher's death anniversary each year. During his stay in Japan, Nyogen was frequently overcome by his emotions, which, after half a century in America, were still lodged in his home country. For the monks at Ryutakuji, the silver-haired, barrel-chested old man with the strangely accented Japanese was a rare attraction, but all were moved by his departing talk.

Returning to the United States, Nyogen spent the last three years of his life in a flat that Mrs. Tanahashi had rented for him in East Los Angeles. He continued to see students until the end, never losing his optimistic down-to-earth manner. Instead of writing the traditional Japanese death poem, Nyogen proved himself to be a true child of the twentieth century—he taped his last words.

Friends in the Dharma, be satisfied with your own head. Do not put any false heads above your own. Then minute after minute, watch your steps closely. Always keep your head cold and your feet warm. These are my last words to you.... The funeral must be performed in the simplest way. A few friends who live nearby may attend it quietly. Those who know how to recite sutras may murmur the shortest one. That will be enough. Do not ask a priest or anyone to make a long service and speech and have others yawn.... Remember me as a monk, and nothing else. I do not belong to any sect or cathedral. None of them should send me a promoted priest's rank or anything of that sort. I like to be free from such trash and die happily.

The monk Nyogen Senzaki died on 7 May 1958. The funeral service went the way he had envisioned it. Only the "few people who live nearby" turned out, enough to fill the halls, side rooms, and every inch of space. His ashes were divided and interred in Hawaii, Japan, California, and New York.

It is not easy to characterize Nyogen Senzaki's teaching. First and foremost, he taught by his own example and was keenly aware that he was only an introductory Zen instructor in his adopted country. He used the three elements of all Rinzai teachers—lectures, zazen, and interviews—to convey the "Zen of Soyen Shaku."

Being both extremely practical and humble, Nyogen could adjust the most difficult and theoretical Buddhist concepts to the potential of his audience, always offering Zen stories and concrete examples to make his point. Widely read and well schooled in the cultural background of his Western audience, he always alluded to common points of reference that would focus the attention of his students. The topics of his lectures were wide ranging, but most of them presented basic Zen Buddhist concepts like zazen, *satori*, karma, sangha, Dharma, and so forth. Nyogen frequently emphasized that Zen was not a religion based on faith, nor was it some sort of speculative philosophy. "It is not enough," Nyogen said, "to tell people that it is possible to become Buddha. What Zen actually does is to produce Buddhas.... Zen is something that must be experienced, not explained. Scientific knowledge is gained and developed by syllogism; but Zen, because it is based solely on intuition, has no need for such a roundabout method. Zen is the actualization of the unselfish life."

There was nothing miraculous about Zen and enlightenment, nobody should expect to emerge as a person with supernatural powers. He railed against what he called "Indian fakirs" who had come to the West and performed all kinds of miracles.

Some Americans pay a good sum of money to learn diverse methods of meditation from so-called Indian "teachers." Some of them give imaginary names to their own bodies, and believe that each part of them develops, meditation after meditation, until Kundalini, the highest stage, is attained. It is like a good card game of solitaire. You can play it by yourself as long as you like. Your physical organs, your stomach and others, however, go on to work constantly in spite of naming them. Besides, your husband or wife will return from their work. If you do not prepare the dinner for two, meditation or no meditation, some "kick" is coming to you just the same.

According to Nyogen Senzaki, there was no way to dispense with karma, the law of causation. Even passing a thousand koans would not turn "a blonde into a brunette." The true teaching of Zen was that every member of the phenomenal world manifests the glory of the noumenon, of *shunyata*, each in its own natural way. If one wished to attain supernatural powers, one had better stop the study of Zen, since it would be a waste of time and effort. "Look at me," Senzaki would say, "I have been studying and practicing Zen meditation for more than forty years, yet I cannot show you the slightest sign of any miracle!"

Nyogen felt that religious institutions and sects were interested in perpetuating this myth of "specialness" in order to wield power and control the behavior of the common people. In Japan, especially during the years immediately preceding the Russo-Japanese War, he had seen how State Shinto and Buddhism had been used to activate the religious fervor of the people for the business of killing and destruction. He resolved never to "belong" to any sect or make himself dependent on a religious institution. No religion could ever claim to possess the Truth, all were like flowers in a garden, manifesting one particular aspect of the human experience. Commenting on a koan whose central image was the ocean, he said, "If anyone makes demarcation foolishly, thinking that he alone has the right view of 'water,' who should not pity him for his ignorance? There are many schools, monasteries, and sects, each considering their own teaching as a lake, rather than a bay, forgetting the inlet to the ocean of Dharma, the universal truth."

Narrow sectarian activities were anathema to this unconventional monk, especially when they were elevated to "holy teachings" recorded for the "salvation" of humankind. "Zen teachers live in this world to take off burdens from their pupils' shoulders," Senzaki insisted, "not to leave beautiful records or romantic anecdotes." After his lectures he always urged his students to "forget everything I said," and find their own inner guide. For this reason, one had to be simple and compassionate, always keeping the well-being of others in mind.

When my master was alive, I asked him to excuse me from all official ranks and titles of our church, and allow me to walk freely in the streets of the world. I do not wish to be called Reverend, Bishop, or by any other church title. To be a member of the great American people and walk any stage of life as I please is honorable enough for me. I want to be an American Hotei, a happy Jap in the streets.

Nyogen's clothing was always tweedy and rumpled; for Zen meetings he would simply wear a robe over his street clothes. As soon as someone would give him money, he either used it to pay the rent for his various "floating zendos" or he would save it for Mrs. Tanahashi to "repay her for her kindness." In the spirit of a true Mahayana Buddhist, a bodhisattva who has the well-being of others in mind, Nyogen never tired of reminding his students that his "Mentorgarten Zen" movement taught nothing but "to calm yourself and to control your breathing, until you become others and others become you." Speaking out against the idea of gradualism in Soto Zen, Senzaki pointed to the possibility of self-actualization right here and now, without any thought of a goal or an end state. "There is no graduation in Zen. Each of us takes a vow to enlighten all sentient beings and, as these are countless, so our vows are endless. From eternity to eternity, Buddhists work to enlighten others, all for one and one for all."

As a method, Nyogen stressed the importance of meditation under the guidance of a good teacher. Having people sit on a chair for only fifteen minutes per zazen period, he taught his students to "regulate your breath and work on your koan!" Once again matching the method with the needs and capacities of his students, Nyogen sometimes dared to change traditional koans, or to make up new ones, which, as he felt, would serve his American sangha better. He highly esteemed the tradition of Christian mystics, especially German representatives like Johannes Tauler and Richard of St. Victor. Lighting on a famous passage of the German mystic Meister Eckhart, Senzaki created the koan, "The eye with which I see God is the very same eye with which God sees me. Show me that eye!" Other koans were, "After you enter your house, then let the house enter into you," or, "You and I met each other many millions of years ago. Now tell me where we have met!"

The true object of zazen, according to Senzaki, was not to have any "object." In this practice of nondualism, one had only to devote oneself to the task at hand, whether it was counting one's breath or working on a koan. *Satori* was not a mere negation, only a letting go of all clinging, even the clinging to "negation" or the experience of *shunyata*. "Don't draw a picture of the everlasting Buddha on the blackboard of your dualistic mind," he warned. "Look at the world, there is an ocean of Buddhas around you." Always addressing his students and audience as "fellow students" or "bodhisattvas," Nyogen indicated with absolute certainty that everyone was already a bodhisattva, ready to realize this fact and then move to help others. His uncompromising nondualism refused to draw a line between "Zen activities" and "ordinary daily activities."

> I have no such funny business as preaching Zen. Whatever I said passed away before you recorded it. You only caught my yawns and coughs.... If I serve you a cup of tea and say, "This is a symbol of Zen," none of you, the students of Zen of the Mentorgarten, will enjoy such a lukewarm beverage.

Nyogen's Zen, like Bankei's teaching of the Unborn in the here and now, emphasized bringing forth the Zen mind in daily activities, unobstructed by thoughts of "specialness" or "religious activity." It was the mind of this very moment that manifested itself in the myriad things of the universe.

> What is this mind that perceives the moon? Zen has a shortcut answer to this question. For the moment you formulate this question, you are already just a second too late. Thinking of the question, you are too late to find the answer. If you think and speak nothing, on the other hand, you are too early. So what can you do?

Loving his independence, the life of a "true man without rank," Nyogen taught the importance of what he called "free-thinking." It was essential to become a confident person who has learned "to stand on one's own feet." Always encouraging questions, he pointed to the strength and power dormant in every person, regardless of talent, physical appearance, or mental sharpness.

Buddhism counsels independence of thought. Buddha inaugurated a religion which, instead of forcing the mind to remain within the boundaries of narrow creeds, actually encourages free-thinking. The system the Buddha formulated explained the whole reason of things, throwing a new and startling light on the mystery of life and death. No longer a baffling riddle, life becomes a wonderful gift that each man may shape for himself as he will. He may ruin his life by wrongdoing, or he may make it a beautiful thing. Man is master of himself and his fate. He himself holds the key to the mystery of life.

This self-confidence combined with compassion was the hallmark of the mature Zen person. Nyogen never forgot to stress the importance of the "whole person beyond sex," someone who had learned to realize male qualities as well as female qualities. Since Nyogen never knew the tenderness of a mother's love, he successfully developed this love in himself. Like Ikkyu, Nyogen, too, loved children. He rejected the idea that discipline, punishment, or harsh words were the right way to educate the young; in their place he bestowed love and taught with a respectful leniency that aimed at a mutually beneficial interaction, rather than the usual adult-child one-way street. He never tired of telling anecdotes

about the years when, as a young monk in charge of a kindergarten, he'd forgotten himself in the joyful screams and wild play
of children, enjoying the happiest time of his life.

> When I was a young monk in Japan, being in charge of a
> kindergarten, I used to play with the children and be
> defeated purposely in a game of wrestling. I had no wish to
> cheat them, but I simply enjoyed being defeated to encour-
> age the children.

Nyogen Senzaki held the highest hopes for the development of
Zen practice in America. Having read the major American
philosophers and educators, he had acquainted himself thoroughly with American culture. Finding American secularism
especially compatible with his anticlericalism, Nyogen admired
American "free-thinkers" like Thomas Paine, Ralph Waldo Emerson, and William James. The latter was a special favorite of the old
monk, who called James's philosophy of practicality the "gospel
of energy." He felt that Zen and American pragmatism had much
in common, since only the daily, practical life, "without great miracles," could reveal the wonders of eating corn flakes in the
morning and catching a bus to work. Resonating with the sen-
timents of freedom and equality that made Americans "natural
Zen students," Nyogen pointed to eight aspects of American life
and character that made the country a fertile ground for Zen.

1. American philosophy is practical.
2. American life does not cling to formality.
3. The majority of Americans are optimists.
4. Americans love nature.

5. They are capable of simple living, being both
   practical and efficient.
6. Americans consider true happiness to lie in
   universal brotherhood.
7. The American conception of ethics is rooted in
   individual morality.
8. Americans are rational thinkers.

Nyogen's depiction of the American national character may not hold true with the passing of the forties and fifties, but his emphasis on American pragmatism is certainly valid today. "American pragmatism," Nyogen would insist, "is but another name for one manifestation of the sparkling rays of Zen in the actual, practical world."

With the same vigor that he defended American culture as "ideal" for the development of Zen, he would condemn formalized Japanese "cathedral" Zen as "hollow, dead, and meaningless." Having witnessed the "Shintoization" of Buddhism and the clinging of the Buddhist clergy to their social status rather than to the teachings of the Buddha, Nyogen's criticisms were harsh and unrelenting. "It is a pity," Nyogen said, "for Zen in Japan to make connections with churches and cathedrals. Properly speaking, they are in opposition to Zen in every respect. There should be no bishops or archbishops in Zen. They all carry clumsy old sticks which were never used to climb mountains....Those priests imitate old symbols of Zen with them. They have no Zen."

Bemoaning the "end of Zen" in Japan and praising the Zen of his late teacher Soyen Shaku, Nyogen wrote a Chinese poem one New Year's Day.

One hundred thousand Bonzes of Japan are intoxi-
cated with sake, on this New Year's Day.
Alone, Brother Soyen is sober, nothing being able to
tempt him.
I lay a lamp on the sill of my window and pine for
him, from this side of the ocean.
He must be very happy when the plum blossoms her-
ald the coming spring!

Nyogen's Zen was the gentle stream that touched the life of
many practitioners both in the United States and in Japan, helping to implant genuine practice in foreign soil. As Robert Aitken
pointed out, Senzaki's "Mentorgarten Zen" has many descendants. After Nyogen's death, Nakagawa Soen Roshi took on
many "Mentorgarten" students himself, or urged them to continue their training with similarly pro-Western Zen teachers, like
Hakuun Yasutani Roshi or Yamada Koun Roshi. The Diamond
Sangha in Hawaii, the Zen Center of Los Angeles, and the Zen
Studies Society in New York all can trace their heritage to the
untiring efforts of Nyogen Senzaki. He never proposed to be a
"founding patriarch" or a "venerable teacher." He just wanted to
provide an opportunity for practice to anyone who was interested in Zen. If his guests wished to meditate, he would show
them how. If they wished to study the scriptures, he would assist
them. If they wished to take the vows to keep the precepts, he
would give them a *jukai* ceremony. Like a storehouse of ancient
treasures that opens by itself, Nyogen would simply "be there."

Fascinated by the simplicity and stark beauty of plants, Senzaki
loved to compare himself to a "homeless mushroom." In one passage he encompassed his whole teaching.

My ideal life is to become a useless mushroom, having no attractive flowers or bothersome stems or leaves. When you start liking me too much, I will disappear from you. I am not like some other religious workers who send out reports to the cathedrals and to fellow workers, and advertise how splendidly they are doing their parts. In fact, I have no cathedral to which I belong. I have no fellow workers as no-work is the work of Zen.

8

Soen: The Master of Play

Nakagawa Soen Roshi was an enigma. The details of his life, like the story *Rashomon*, vary with each witness: he was born in Formosa, he was born near Hiroshima; he was a teetotaler, he was an alcoholic; he was manic depressive, he had an accident that affected his brain; he worked on koans with Western students, he never accepted Western students for koan practice…and on and on it goes. He was tiny, but seemed enormous; he had a booming voice and the light step of a ballet dancer; he was entirely Western in his tastes; and so completely an oriental Zen master that he seemed to have stepped out of an ancient koan collection.

Perle Besserman met Soen Roshi in 1982, on his last visit to the United States, two years before he died:

We took tea together, he stirring the bitter green powder, and I pouring the boiling water and passing him chocolate chip cookies on a platter. He told stories, endless stories…about wandering in China, pointing out to me that we were drinking from none other than the precious bowl of master Rinzai himself! Soen was antic, as my Zen friends had warned me. In the middle of tea, he ordered his Dharma successors to massage him, one *roshi* at his head and neck and the other at his feet. All the while he went on talking, charming his audience with his tales, compelled—like Scheherazade—to spin stories. Even then, as he neared the end of his life, Soen Roshi was himself both hero and narrator of a fantastic story, one that he had been improvising for half a century.

In 1905, two years before Nakagawa Soen was born to a physician army officer and his wife in a small town near Hiroshima, the Japanese had conquered the Russians and extended their empire as far as the Liaotung peninsula and Korea. The "Meiji Miracle" coincided with the birth of this Zen prodigy, the emblematic triumph of Japanese nationalism, and the Dharma spreading westward. The Sino-Japanese War in 1895 had already convinced the nation that it was now the wellspring of culture for all of East Asia, a modernizing force for establishing Western civilization among the backward peoples of China and Korea. Nakagawa Soen personified this interesting amalgam of East and West, finding his Zen roots in ancient Chinese culture (living with his family in Formosa while a very young boy), and also developing a Western persona in his love for the arts and civilization of Europe, and the anarchistic individualism of America.

Japanese politics and Japanese Zen were never democratic. Influenced by oligarchy, emperor worship, and the samurai code, both moved inevitably toward the fascism of the 1930s, which ultimately brought Japan's defeat in World War II. There had been several short-lived attempts at establishing a party democracy, but the universal manhood suffrage established in 1925 resulted in two major parties whose leaders represented powerful monopolies and were virtually as unavailable to the common people as the Tokugawa shogunate had been two centuries before. Socialists and Christians, artists, intellectuals, and anarchists had vied with each other in search of a dissenting voice. But all were silenced in 1910, when a group of radical anarchists caught in a plot to assassinate the emperor were executed.

World War I brought Japan its first heady wave of economic success. *Zaibatsu*, the powerful monopolies linking ruling families like Mitsui and Mitsubishi, controlled the country's politics, its bureaucracy, and its religious hierarchy. The Russian Revolution provoked a tiny resurgence of Japanese radicalism, even a few strikes in the cities, but Japanese society did not lend itself to socialism. Its Confucian structure and its Tokugawa-inspired hierarchy were too entrenched. Farmers remained clan oriented and reactionary in their politics; even urban laborers revered the emperor as a divine being; and factory workers were content to live under traditional paternalistic company codes that are still in place in Japan today. The built-in tendency to accept and submit to authority gave way to an occasional rice riot, but these were no more effective in provoking mass social change than they had been during Ikkyu's times.

Alienation was the cultural hallmark of Japan in the 1920s and 30s, and Nakagawa Soen grew up as a poet among its disaffected artists and intellectuals. Novelists were seeking for individuality and psychological identity in the most rigidly conformist society of the modern world. Romantic lifestyles, poetry, music, painting, and philosophy flourished in the demimonde of misfits. Continuously at odds over "Eastern spirituality and Western materialism," Japanese intellectuals of the post–World War I period immersed themselves in a sea of popular culture imported from the West:

bars, cafes, American cinema, dances, music, even architecture changed the face of Tokyo after the great earthquake of 1923. Baseball, golf, and tennis swept Japan then, as they did once again after World War II. In the midst of this flood of Western culture, Soen the high school boy, enthralled by European classical music, persuaded a friend to chip in with him and buy a recording of Beethoven's Ninth Symphony that set his "body shivering for three days afterwards."

With the great stockmarket crash, Japan moved away from coop-eration with the West and toward a more forceful nationalist approach that led to the usurpation of Manchuria in 1933. Mili-taristic, right-wing behavior was the order of the day. Using the emperor as the symbol of their platform, ultranationalists terrorized even the powerful capitalists and their political pawns. All pretense at democratic party government came to an end in May 1932, when a group of young naval officers assassinated the prime min-ister and assumed control of the country. By 1940, in the "name of national unity," fascism was in the ascendant, and militarism, *bushido*, its voice. As in the past, this old samurai spirit could not tolerate "foreigners"—except for the Germans, with whom the militarists signed a pact in hope of achieving their ultimate goal of annexing China, Southeast Asia, Australia, and New Zealand.

Soen, the army officer's son, applied for military service and was rejected for a mistakenly diagnosed punctured eardrum. But by then there were two Soens: one a monk ordained in 1930, immediately after graduating from Tokyo University, already a celebrated haiku poet and specialist in Japanese literature and Shakespeare; the other, his widowed mother's son, a traditional samurai willing to die for his country. To his mother's dismay, Soen the monk triumphed.

1945 saw the defeat of Japan and the exhaustion of its people. Postwar society was pervaded by a GI culture of films, chocolates, strip shows, and an unprecedented display of consumer goods. The United States was no longer the enemy, but the "favorite foreign country" of the Japanese people. General MacArthur hoped to turn Japan into the "Switzerland of the Far East," a demilitarized zone with a democratic constitution, decentralization of the national police force and educational system, and an end to emperor worship and the samurai code. What resulted is the stuff of current newspaper headlines: another "Japanese miracle," an economic-industrial boom that thrust the vanquished far ahead of their occupiers.

Immediately after the war there was a rush for translations of Western literature; Japanese intellectuals now turned to Western existentialism, the modish philosophy of the forties and fifties, and, finally, to a new form of dissolute romanticism bordering on nihilism. The artist, the individualist, was still seeking a place in Japanese society; but there was no room.

Even today, the Japanese still live in groups, marry in groups, bathe, work, and vacation in groups. They are still wedded to the idea of clan loyalty, and many of them still believe that they are a superior breed of being surrounded by barbarians; only now they enjoy barbarian goods, films, music, food, and lifestyles. Zen monasteries continue to maintain their traditional ties to the powerful and wealthy, and their barriers against Westerners. Celebrated roshis publicly insist that Westerners are incapable of experiencing *satori*, and those who have gone abroad to spread the Dharma among Westerners are largely regarded as outcasts. Soen Roshi was among the first of this new breed of postwar wanderers. His life and teaching represent the quintessential Japanese dilemma between duty *(giri)* and the pull of his own emotions *(ninjo)*. His story is itself a modern Noh drama of conflicting loyalties, poetic vision, and worldly betrayal, a struggle that split him apart.

Born on 19 March 1907, Soen was the eldest of three boys. When he was twelve, his father died, leaving his young mother a widow in straitened circumstances. A second tragedy struck when Tamotsu, her middle son, died in childhood. Soen's mother behaved like a very unconventional Japanese woman of the samurai class; she went to work as a midwife, scrimping and saving to support and educate her children herself.

As a boy, Soen was a gifted poet and actor who easily endeared himself to the adults in his life. He exhibited an unusual appreciation of the arts even as a child, and, though he was trained and raised as a samurai and was expected to follow in his father's footsteps, he displayed a yearning for the spiritual life while still in high school. Soen's lifelong friend, Yamada Koun Roshi, entered Tokyo's First High School on the same day. The two boys became roommates, and though Yamada felt they were intimate friends, he was always surprised by Soen's "spiritual" confessions.

> The two of us would often go for a walk around the Hongo neighborhood in the late evening. One night, quite unexpectedly, he said something a trifle frightening. He spoke of how almost every evening he was sitting in zazen on top of the platform of the balancing bars in the sportsground. He said that in fact the previous evening, he had had some kind of spiritual experience. He told me I should never speak of this to anyone. Quite some time later, he gave the interpretation that it should probably be called a "natural self-realization."

At that time, although I did not understand at all, I somehow felt that I had had a glimpse of the deep recesses of his heart.

Soen the high school boy was already engaged in a secret spiritual search for his life's meaning. In an article published after he had become a monk, he describes his freshman year in high school as a period of "searching for something worthwhile to dedicate my life to." He would settle for nothing less than a grand and worthy goal, and was dispirited at finding nothing that met his needs "in the everyday world." Hiding his desperation from Yamada, he buried himself every evening in the library, poring over the works of philosophers like Schopenhauer in search of a purpose. Once, he came upon a page that shocked him.

My mind ceased searching. It became lucid and tranquil. Schopenhauer said, "In the *real* world, it is impossible to attain true happiness, final and eternal contentment. For these are visionary flowers in the air; mere fantasies. In truth they can never be actualized. In fact, they must not be actualized. Why? If such ideas were actualized, the search for the real meaning of our existence would cease. If that happened, it would be the spiritual end of our being, and life would seem too foolish to live."

Schopenhauer led to Zen, and soon, Soen was trying to engage his young friend Yamada in his marvelous find. Handing him an old book by Zen master Hakuin, the *Orategama*, Soen said, "Please try and read this book." Yamada read Hakuin and was excited by Zen, but not enough to join his friend in zazen atop a shaky platform.

The two boys went on to Tokyo University together; Soen majored in Japanese literature and wrote his final thesis on Basho, the Zen haiku poet. He also wrote his own poetry and immersed himself in Buddhist scriptures, the Bible, and Western and Japanese literary classics, while frequenting the theater, listening to Schubert, Beethoven, and Wagner, and joining a circle of friends who were to become the artistic and intellectual elite of modern Japan. At the university, Soen started a small Zen sitting group that is still active today. "I will become a god," he confided to his younger brother Sonow. "After graduation, I will work in society for ten years; for the next ten years I will go to the mountains on retreat and become enlightened; and then I will return once again to society."

Yamada and Soen graduated from the university together in 1930 and temporarily lost touch. One day, Yamada, now a businessman, was informed that he had a guest. Walking into the reception room, he was startled to see his old friend Soen sitting in a chair dressed in monk's robes. "You certainly have changed," he said. Looking at Yamada's spiffy business suit, Soen replied, "You've changed quite a bit, too." Soen had carried his search to its inevitable resolution. Almost immediately after graduating from the university, he had attended a Zen meeting at Shorinji, a monastery headed by Katsube Keigaku Roshi, and, much to his mother's consternation, asked to be ordained on his birthday— no doubt to symbolize his "rebirth." Orchestrating even his ordination, Soen insisted that the ceremony take place at Kogakuji, the monastery of his favorite Zen master, Bassui, whose koan "Who is the master of hearing?" he had been assigned. Following in the legendary footsteps of the esteemed Bassui, he took up residence near Kogakuji, on Dai Bosatsu mountain. Traveling back and forth between his home monastery and Dai Bosatsu mountain, Soen lived the mixed life of the monk and hermit-poet, dedicating himself to zazen, writing articles and verse, fasting or subsisting on wild plants, and bathing in freezing mountain streams. It was here that he was found by peasants one day, half dead from having eaten poisonous mushrooms. His rescuers nursed him back to health and befriended the young poet-monk, providing him from then on with edible food and looking to him as their priest; it was much the same situation enjoyed by Bassui, who had written folk poems for *his* peasant congregation on that same mountain six centuries before.

Once, when accompanying Katsube Roshi on a weekend meditation retreat for Tokyo University students, Soen discovered that he was missing a *kyosaku*, the wooden stick used for "encouraging" sleepy sitters. Hoping to borrow one, he walked over to Hakusan Dojo, a nearby Zen center, and entered in the middle of a Dharma talk given by Yamamoto Gempo Roshi of Ryutakuji monastery in Mishima, an hour's trip from Tokyo. Moved to stay and listen a bit, Soen soon found himself "bathed in a universal ocean of warmth and penetration." Before long, he had become a frequent visitor at Hakusan Dojo, attending Gempo Roshi's talks and enjoying the universal ocean of warmth until one day he heard, "If you practice zazen, it must be *true* practice." Soen felt the roshi had aimed that remark directly at him. When the talk was over, he asked for a private interview and immediately offered to become Gempo Roshi's monk. A true child of Pisces, Soen was as quicksilvery as a carp in a temple pond. On that day, he set the first scene for his free-flowing Zen style, his mercurial mind changes, his dramatic entrances and disappearances.

In 1938, Yamada was transferred to a job in Manchuria, where to his surprise, he again met his old friend Soen, now attendant to Gempo Roshi. The two were on a mission to start a branch of Myoshinji Zen in the Japanese colony. Yamada and Gempo Roshi were nationalists with few reservations about Japanese expansionism. But Soen was impatient with traditional Japanese Zen and its rigidly nationalistic political connections. He told Yamada that he dreamed of creating an antiestablishment practice in the style of Bassui up on Dai Bosatsu mountain. What he did not tell Yamada was that he had already begun to correspond with Nyogen Senzaki in America, and that he was being injected with Senzaki's rebellious "foreign" ideas.

"We used to go for walks together at night," Yamada recalls, "just as we did when we were students. At one point I must have been quibbling about something rather heatedly when [Soen] said, 'Yamada, all you do is argue. Why don't you try sitting?'" That remark prompted Yamada's interest, but several years would pass before he would begin Zen practice and become a roshi himself. "Perhaps," he concludes, "Nakagawa Roshi was too much of a poet."

World War II prevented Soen from meeting Nyogen Senzaki in the flesh; and it was not until 8 April 1948, on the traditional date of Buddha's birthday, that the two actually faced each other on a San Francisco pier. Finding Senzaki's "anticathedral" Zen and the American climate perfectly suited to his own unconventional style, Soen combined the poet, Noh actor, and Zen radical in himself to create an inimitable persona. Here, in the free atmosphere of the American West, he could quote from *Faust* as well as from Hakuin and Bassui in his Zen lectures. Here he could demonstrate Bassui's "master of hearing" in the form of a Noh drama, something the monks back at Ryutakuji would find laughable. Nyogen Senzaki hoped that Soen would remain in the United States and become his successor, but because of Soen's monastic commitments in Japan, the two had to content themselves with frequent traveling visits. Soen maintained his ties with American, European, and Israeli students, traveling between East and West for the next thirty-three years.

In 1950, Gempo Roshi decided to retire and appointed Soen abbot of Ryutakuji. The new abbot was so reluctant to assume the post that he refused to wear the traditional golden regalia during the ceremony and appeared in simple black monk's robes. Moreover, he disappeared from the monastery soon after, leaving Gempo Roshi without an abbot for the inaugural *sesshin*, and forcing the old teacher to stand in for his Dharma heir himself! Only Soen's mother could bring the eccentric young abbot down from his Dai Bosatsu mountain hermitage. Where she was concerned, there was no conflict of loyalty.

Soen's tenure as abbot of Ryutakuji was by no means typical of a traditional Zen abbot. He dressed in the plain robes of a monk, ate his meals in the refectory with his novices, bathed in the communal bath with them, even sat zazen with them. Insisting that he had himself completed "only" the five hundred required koans of Hakuin's curriculum of seventeen hundred Rinzai koans, he visited other notable Zen masters to continue his "polishing." Traveling great distances, he studied with Harada Roshi of Hosshinji, himself a renowned Zen reformer who wedded Rinzai and Soto schools in a new lineage that bemused the Zen establishment and changed the face of Zen practice to this day. Under the influence of Harada in Japan and Senzaki in the United States, Soen soon developed his own amalgam of Zen practice and performance,

using "Namu dai bosa" ("I call upon the name of the great bodhisattva") as a kind of mantra, which he, and his American students
at least, repeated over and over again in a loud shout that cas-
caded into silent meditation. He particularly loved taking students out into nature and shouting this self-styled koan at the
moon, the trees, the sky, and the water.

As an "American Zen master," Soen Roshi could indulge Soen
the performer even as he instructed his students. He wrote haiku
poetry and used it as a teaching tool; he recited Shakespeare along
with Rinzai in his Dharma talks; he visited the great museums of
Europe, and incorporated his growing knowledge of Christian
and Jewish traditions and scripture into his presentation of the
Buddhadharma. As a Japanese monastery abbot, he was, in the
words of D.T. Suzuki, "a rather peculiar fellow." But Soen considered himself "Hakuin's child," and Hakuin, too, had been
thought of as peculiar by the Japanese Zen establishment.

It would appear that Soen's deep attachment to his mother had
left him a perpetual boy, what psychologist Carl Jung would call
a *puer*, the charming eternal child who, like Peter Pan, simply
refuses to grow up. When his mother died in 1962, only a year
after Gempo Roshi, Soen was truly orphaned twice. Gempo
Roshi had often stepped into the breach for his wayward young
successor, and Soen's mother, in a situation unheard of in the long
history of Zen, was firmly established at the monastery, seeing
her son daily, walking with him in the mountains, listening to
their magnificent collection of Western classical music, enter-
taining patrons at tea ceremony, and advising him on all matters.
Thus, women students found Soen the most respectful of Japanese Zen teachers, for he saw them all in an idealized, platonic
light that emanated from his adoration of his mother. This of

course did not endear him with his macho Zen peers; nor did his "effete" love for ceremony, poetry, and art appeal to the rough country novices at Ryutakuji either.

Soen's solitary retreats to Dai Bosatsu mountain increased after his mother's death. In 1965, during one of these long periods of isolation, he slipped from a precipice and suffered a blow to his head. Lying unconscious for three days until he was discovered, Soen Roshi awoke, but as his friend Yamada put it, "he was never the same." Nonetheless, he continued as abbot of Ryutakuji and honorary abbot of Dai Bosatsu monastery in Beecher Lake, New York, and the Jerusalem Zen Society on the Mount of Olives in Israel. He still traveled around the world, held retreats, and gave interviews to his adoring Western students, and he appointed five successors of his own. But by the mid-1970s, Soen was enervated, retreating into isolation for months at a time to escape the pain and disappointment of a dream betrayed, for he had never successfully "spread the Dharma net East and West," as he had once hopefully written. In March 1984, only a few days after his seventy-seventh birthday, while taking a bath at Ryutakuji, Soen Roshi passed quietly from this world.

Soen's teaching style was based entirely on communicating the suchness of the moment. "Only *This, This!*" he would cry, slapping his cushion to illustrate his point. Whether discoursing on Rinzai or dancing under the moon, his single purpose was to lock his students into the reality of immediacy. Robert Aitken Roshi, one of Soen's earliest Western Zen students, wrote, "Soen Roshi was intimately in touch with his Buddhist origins, and as an artist of the body, his way was to act them out, and to encourage others to act them out as well."

Intent on creating an "international Zen," Soen added to his Buddhist origins by taking communion at Saint Patrick's Cathedral in New York and, after donning a black caftan and hat, dancing with Hasidim in Israel. Seeking to combine his artistic gifts, his playful nature, and his role as a Zen teacher, he gathered flute masters, Catholic priests, and street people as players in his elaborate Zen performances. Insisting that the spiritual and physical worlds, the angels, devils, and bodhisattvas were all equally real, he invested every Dharma talk, every retreat and koan interview with the joyful spontaneity of enlightenment. "This world is so wonderful, so Unthinkable and Ungraspable. *What are we touching right here now?*" he would cry, gleefully thumping his cushion.

Just hearing, just dancing, were the rallying cries of his universal brotherhood. He chastised quietists for trying to "empty the mind," and advocated living in the "present mind" instead, without a glimmer of self-conscious spirituality. To expunge the stink of Zen from his students, he even went so far as to place a large pumpkin on his cushion in the *dokusan* room, hiding behind a screen and laughing as they entered and bowed deeply before it. To illustrate the drama of perpetual change, he enacted his Dharma talks behind a red demon mask and played all the parts in his improvised Noh play with his robe pulled up over his head. When Nyogen Senzaki died in 1958, Soen came to California, conducted a *sesshin* in his memory, and gave a brief talk. Then he dispersed part of Senzaki's ashes at the Tassajara monastery in California and conducted a ceremonial dance under the full moon, clapping and singing the Heart Sutra in his friend's honor.

No form of celebration was inappropriate. Dancing as meditation "should be full of Dharma delight; we should feel so full of gratitude that we cannot sit still, that we naturally start dancing.... Both are universal, dancing and sitting." Embodying Bodhidharma's famous Zen motto, "Nothing holy," Soen conducted tea ceremony with coffee or soda pop, ate cherry blossoms in front of the Capitol in Washington, D.C., and discoursed on the virtues of "shitting" as an equally important form of Zen as "sitting."

> Ordinary is extraordinary.... Dramas all have only one point...it is to understand this Great Matter...to understand this, to realize this, to actualize this in everyday life, in ordinary life, in every ordinary life. There is no need to go to Kabuki. Of course it is wonderful; I admire it very much. But the drama is not only with Rinzai and Obaku and Bokushu, and Noh actors, and wonderful New York actors and actresses. Even eating, cooking, and sleeping—each deed of your everyday life is nothing else but this Great Matter.

Soen's insistence that the "real" and "spiritual" worlds were one and the same extended also to his definition of birth and death. The only difference between these two conditions, he said, lay in the names we used to express them. Otherwise, even birth and death were the same.

> To die is to join the majority. Some of us will go to a dark, dismal world, some to a beautiful, transparent world, some to a noisy, pilgrimaging world. But we will all join the majority. Congratulations! For this reason we celebrate death-day, together with birth-day.

For him no distinctions existed even in the "Miserable karma relations, world war...miserable cruel karma relations," which could be immediately transformed into "wonderful Dharma relations" with the mere recognition of the interdependence of things. Nothing but this cup, this drinking, this bird chirping…nothing else but this right here now! He warned students against self-conscious holiness, "neurotic mindfulness," using his eccentric versions of the tea ceremony to show the radiant simplicity inherent in "just boiling water and making tea, just drinking it. Nothing else."

In the middle of a Dharma talk he would spontaneously organize a bowing session, encouraging students by bowing in front of them, assuring them that "each one of you is a bodhisattva." Then, directing them to bow to each other, wife and husband, friend and stranger, he exhorted everyone to "bow to the living bodhisattva that is each of you." Words were never sufficient to communicate the Great Matter. Only experience conveyed it, only action and being. The Ten Commandments and the Buddhist precepts themselves were simply words. "Don't, don't, don't see them as bindings! They make us free…they are important. But do not be bound up by commandments. *Everything* is *yourself*. Everything is *myself*. Each of you is master of his whole universe."

Contact with his students at the Jerusalem zendo gave him ever new insights and symbols for teaching. Even the most dualistic religious archetypes suited his purpose.

My friends tell me there are eight gates in the Jerusalem wall. One of the gates is the Never-Open Gate. The Golden Gate. The Messiah will appear, riding a donkey, and go down the hillside. All the spirits sleeping under the tombs will wake and follow him through the Never-Open Gate, into the temple…. Never-Opened Gate is opened! Do you believe this? From the beginning the door is open. It cannot open more.

Nothing was sacrosanct. Not even zazen.

Meditation itself is not Zen. Zen is meditation, but it is also thinking, eating, drinking, sitting, standing, shitting, peeing—all of these are nothing else but Zen.... Zazen is sitting Zen. But this is not the Zen. Don't be mistaken about this point.

The enlightenment experience itself disappeared and had to be recalled over and over again. "There's no end; no graduation. Even Buddha...is training, training, training...every day." But students were not to make a fetish of their practice: "When meditating on something, just meditate on it. When cooking, just cook. When drinking, just drink. Nothing else but this.... In the midst of all our doing, there is this *doing* nothing."

Every occasion was rich with possibilities for revealing the Dharma, particularly the everyday variety, the kind that usually makes spiritual people squeamish. Once, he opened a talk with a story about a cockroach.

Cockroach was my pet. Cockroach is living with his whole heart, with his whole might. Wonderful wonderful Zen! More Zen than you.... Better than human beings. Human beings are more or less masters of the earth now—well, only human beings can get true enlightenment, but disease and cruelty...but this I skip for now.... Anyway, in my room where there is not food or anything, a big cockroach came to me for the first time. Probably the king of cockroaches.

And he sat by me…I talked with him of wonderful matters. The next night too, he came. Every night. And then, he stopped coming.

Even a cockroach was a worthy conversationalist in a world where:

All beings are flowers
Blooming
In a blooming universe.

Nyogen Senzaki once told an American student, "Soen Roshi is pure love." Not only cockroaches, but ferocious dogs and unquiet babies were hypnotized by his presence. Like the Pied Piper, he could draw a group of hardened New York Zen sitters into a "sutra-chanting contest" and defuse their competitiveness with the laughing assertion that there were no winners, for "everyone is best!" Hidden in the sleeves of his robe were fruits, flowers, souvenirs picked up on a walk in the park, and he dispensed these gifts freely. Once, when a woman student offered him a Buddhist piece of sculpture that he had admired, he thanked her for it and said, "But don't be angry when I give it away. Someone else might like it."

Nature's oddities fascinated him. During a retreat in Connecticut, he woke several students in the middle of the night, and, with his finger on his lips, took them downstairs in silence. Gathering them before a windowsill and motioning for a woman with a flashlight to shine it there, he pointed to a night-blooming cereus in a pot. Ruth Lilienthal, one of Soen's oldest students, was present. She recalls, "The air above the open-mouthed flower was radiant with energy. Tears come even now as I remember this exquisite, wordless birth." At that same retreat he conducted student interviews in a domed pup tent, crawling in on all fours, and urging his students to do the same. Nothing holy.

But back in Japan, where he was Zen master to the imperial prince and the prime minister, Soen Roshi was "every inch" a traditional abbot. Which was the real Soen, the mischievous imp who played Beethoven's Ninth Symphony at meditation retreats, the moonstruck dancer who erased all hierarchical differences by defining all humans as "members of the same nosehole society," the teacher who led a student out of the interview room to view a magnificent sunset, the poet whose material was everyday life, the artist who crafted enlightened beings—or the somber, traditional Zen abbot, national teacher to the imperial house?

In search of the "real" Soen Roshi, Perle Besserman made her way to Ryutakuji in 1983.

I stood with my gift of strawberries on a freezing February day, waiting for his attendant monk to give me the signal to see him. The monks in the kitchen tittered. One, in faltering English, said, "Why you want to see Soen Roshi? He crazy," and he made circling motions with his finger at his temple to illustrate the point. The strawberries were accepted but no invitation came. The attendant monk, a girlish fellow with long, tapered fingers and ash-colored eyes, only shook his head. Soen Roshi was not seeing anyone. He'd gone back into one of his long, hermetic retreats by locking himself into his little cottage on the monastery grounds. Rumor had it that he'd grown his hair down to his shoulders, that he had long, clawlike fingernails, that he was wetting his pants and had to be tied to the bed. Even in hiding, Soen's life had assumed Shakespearean proportions.

One day, as I was sweeping the balcony around the monastery's main hall, I heard the strains of a Schubert sonata coming from the little mountain hut where he lived. Maybe now, I thought, maybe he'll come out now. But he didn't. I hoped he might come out with the full moon. But he never showed himself once in the two months I spent there.

The head monk at Ryutaku-ji had said it was Soen Roshi who inspired him to finish with his Marxism, his secular studies at the university, and become a monk. "He was powerful, magnetic."

"Yes he was," I replied, remembering the tea and Rinzai's bowl, and the chocolate-chip cookies, and the booming magician's voice weaving stories.

Was Soen Roshi ultimately "ineffective as a Zen teacher," as some of his students later claimed? Was he in fact "too eccentric," too much the "poet" and not enough the roshi? Those successors who seek to perpetuate the "Soen mystique," even going so far as to canonize him only five years after his death, were themselves often among his greatest detractors while he lived. Several of his closest students attribute his breakdown to the profound sense of betrayal he suffered at the hands of his principal successors. What place has Zen for such antics as Soen's? Where to draw the line between being a Crazy Cloud and just plain "crazy"? Perhaps only artists and children can answer. For Soen spoke most intimately to all who refused to grow up, who sought to "play," "dance," and "wonder." His real successors are not the black-robed roshis but the Zen musicians and writers, the painters and tea ceremony masters, the little band of Dharma players for whom "singing and dancing are the voice of the Law."

One winter, when he was living alone and happy in an unheated cottage in the Catskills, bathing in icy Beecher Lake and eating what plants he could find in the snow, Soen scratched a poem into a wooden board that read:

> Ten years' searching in the deep forest
> Today great laughter at the edge of the lake.

That laughter is his Zen legacy.

Epilogue:
From "Crazy Cloud" Zen
to "Grassroots" Zen

Thanks to nonconformist twentieth-century Zen masters like Nakagawa Soen and Nyogen Senzaki, the Crazy Cloud spirit has found a welcome home in the West. However, before we can speak about the efficacy of their radical Zen teachings for Westerners in the twenty-first century, we must first explore the effects of hierarchical Zen, and of Japanese Zen in particular. While significantly decreasing overall, a number of major cultural incompatibilities still cause problems for Western practitioners today. These sticking points include attitudes toward the role of the teacher and the religious hierarchy; the status of women in Zen and questions of sex, celibacy, and family; and the relationship of Zen to ethics, as we translate them into sociopolitical involvement, and the traditional "flight from the world" associated with monastic Buddhism in general.

In order for a new religion to take root in foreign soil, certain charismatic role players or very specific cultural trends must appear to spread the word. In this fashion, Buddhism easily took hold in societies whose caste structures provided a "royal road" for its entry. Appealing to kings and emperors, shoguns and warriors, this portable religion was perpetuated by indigenous Asian figures who painted it in local colors. Nonetheless, Buddhism remained unmistakably Buddhist in its religious content, ritual, and practice. After centuries, the feudal context of the faith was forgotten, and an evolving society became its own religious arbiter. The best example for this absorbed state of Buddhism is Japan, which is so drenched in Zen that the words "Japan" and "Zen" are often used interchangeably. Art, literature, the emperor, priests, and the warrior code are still universal cue-givers in Japan, and, although the practice and influence of Zen as a religion is diminishing from year to year, the Japanese cultural matrix continues to reinforce cues reflective of the Buddhist experience.

The situation in the West is radically different. In the United States, where Jeffersonian democratic ideals and a puritan entrepreneurial spirit form the cultural matrix, secularization has undermined the validity of any hierarchy at all. Spiritual cues are mediated by advertisements, TV, film, and the Internet, which tend to level culture for mass consumption. "Royal" individuals or institutions are irrelevant in the "democracy of the many." Thus, traditional Zen practice, with its roshi, or venerable teacher, at the top of the pyramid, is antithetical to new generations of Americans and, increasingly, Europeans and Asians, whose scorn for authority of any kind would preclude any form of teacher worship. Today's children, from very early on, are encouraged to form their own opinions and to express them eloquently and critically. The uniqueness of each and every individual, and his or her freedom, are values that present a major obstacle to patriarchal expressions of absolute faith in "the old man." The degree to which a Zen teacher's words and actions are subject to student criticism is still, however, an unresolved issue. Even the most egalitarian Zen teacher remains hampered by the authoritative forms that he or she has inherited from the very heart of Buddhism itself. After all, it is only the roshi who can confirm a "true" experience of enlightenment, and only the roshi who determines who his or her successors will be—sometimes in a very arbitrary and autocratic way. As an expert in "ultimate questions," the roshi is expected to deal effortlessly with mundane earthly concerns.

Thus, some Zen teachers have even allowed their spiritual expertise to encroach on nondharmic aspects of their students' lives, giving opinions and guidance on matters of business and family affairs. This creates an uncomfortable paradox; for if the roshi is "just a normal guy or gal," then the spiritual weight of the tradition and title are superfluous, even ridiculous in the context of everyday life in an increasingly egalitarian world. It is "specialness" after all that makes a roshi, but being "special" doesn't square well with democratic ideals. This conflict between hierarchy and individualism is in great part responsible for the confusion experienced in many Western Zen centers when students put their teachers in a double bind by demanding that they be "authentic" Zen masters on the one hand, and "the guy or gal next door" on the other. It is impossible to maintain the unquestioned authority of a Zen teacher in an egalitarian society.

In an effort to democratize Zen, several second-generation American practitioners have done away with the trappings of their monastic inheritance, such as Japanese sutra recitation, bowls and chopsticks, formal robes, and traditional Japanese terminology, including even the title roshi. In their place we see "hiking retreats," New England–style town meetings with full membership voting and consensus, the separation of administrative and spiritual parts of the Zen center, and job rotation that includes the teacher in even the most menial tasks. Sometimes even the word *Zen* itself is dropped in favor of the nonsectarian term *meditation*.

Vertical hierarchies collapse into horizontally shaped communities, and even Zen centers that once prided themselves on being "traditional," that is, Japanese, Chinese, or Korean, have acknowledged the need for greater distribution of power, individual initiative, and a family-oriented practice for laypeople.

It has become clear that this process will continue throughout the next decades, further changing the face of Zen in the West, and reflecting the democratic spirit of a Buddhist practice that is being forced to accommodate itself to its new home in order to survive. Perhaps the most significant example of this trend has been the influential role of women. Outside of Asia at least, the male domination of Zen has diminished. The denial of female sexuality is no longer acceptable to a community of practitioners who have no cultural connection to the samurai code. Language, therefore, changes to include students of both sexes, new rituals replace the old, and sexual harassment by charismatic teachers is no longer tolerated. Nothing in the last century has changed our male-dominated Western society as profoundly as the feminist struggle for equal rights in all domains. Although far from over, the struggle has placed women at the forefront of a social revolution that can no longer be ignored. The Judeo-Christian religions of the West have had to face up to the new status of women, but only a small portion of this has recently filtered into traditional Asian Buddhist models. For many people, Zen still represents a bastion of male supremacy, a warrior religion set on combat, bravery, and death. Zen practitioners for more than five centuries have been drilled in throwing away such "negative" feminine qualities as emotional openness, self-regard, and sentiment. The very stuff of Zen practice is male: koans that grew out of spontaneous dialogues fashioned between monks; heroes who best their less enlightened rivals in Dharma combat; and a good deal of beating and stick wielding. No matter how you look at it, Zen has been an unremittingly male practice, since it was conceived and handed down almost exclusively by men for almost twenty-five hundred years. We should not deceive ourselves into thinking that the Buddha's democratization of the Indian caste system included making women roshi. Most Japanese Zen masters who came West in the late 1950s and early 60s perpetuated this male model of spiritual soldiers who would penetrate delusions and win the war for enlightenment. But what they encountered was a sangha whose members were fifty percent female, and they were not prepared.

In the 1980s, after a series of sex scandals in various American Zen centers threatened the stability of Zen institutions in the West, both male and female Zen students started experimenting with new forms of practice. By the early 90s, influenced by its growing feminist leadership, the Zen monastic model had gradually been replaced by a more inclusive form of practice combining focused meditation with the concerns of laypeople in a rapidly globalizing high-tech world. Emphasis on family, jobs, disability, and aging were taken just as seriously as monastic routines—some zendos even going so far as to incorporate child care into meditation retreat schedules and provide ramps for sitters in wheelchairs.

Another aspect of changing trends in both Asian and Western Zen has been an increasing emphasis on social justice. Until very recently, the Zen hierarchy in Japan was either silent in matters of social and political engagement or stridently militaristic. The apparent nihilism of the sixteenth-century swordmaster and Zen teacher Takuan fueled Japanese militarism in Zen terms that, despite reformist efforts at demilitarizing the practice, still ring loudly in the ears of nationalists today.

> The uplifted sword has no will of its own, it is all of emptiness. It is like a flash of lightning. The man who is about to be struck down is also of emptiness, as is the one who wields the sword.... Do not get your mind stopped with the sword you raise; forget about what you are doing, and strike the enemy. Do not keep your mind on the person before you. They are all of emptiness, but beware of your mind being caught in emptiness.

This worldview was reflected in those jingoistic Zen masters who supported the Russo-Japanese War, and those who contemplated suicide after Japan's defeat in World War II. The Zen emphasis on *bushido*, the warrior code, which justifies breaking the Buddhist precept of not killing and glorifies militarism, has led many Western Zen practitioners to ask themselves whether there is an ethical system inherent in Japanese Zen at all. Commenting on Takuan's amorality, the American Zen teacher Robert Aitken wrote:

> The separation of the absolute from the relative and the treatment of the absolute as something impenetrable may be good Hinduism, but it is not the teaching of the Buddha, for whom absolute and relative were inseparable except when necessary to highlight them as aspects of a unified reality.... The vow of Takuan Zenji to save all beings did not encompass the one he called "the enemy."

Does the strongly rooted Judeo-Christian ethic of the West point to the inevitable "pacification" of Zen? Though movement toward a more engaged, peace-promoting form of Zen has been slow and is far from all-inclusive, many American, European, Asian, and Latin American students have begun to see their practice as a blend of spiritual insight and concrete social action within the sphere of historical events. The American tradition of a separation of church and state has never adversely affected strong socio-political movements that took off from religiously motivated morality and a sense of social justice. American Protestantism, with its inner-worldly engagement and its action-oriented life of "good works," is beginning to color an otherwise neutral Zen stance. Several Zen centers worldwide are actively engaged in ecumenical social work, linking up with Jews, Catholics, and Protestants, as well as with other Buddhist groups, to engage in ethical activism of the kind that evolved during the Vietnam War in Southeast Asia. Focusing specifically on problems of homelessness, environmental issues, disarmament, and racism, several Zen centers have successfully incorporated social action programs into their formal meditation practice.

Typically, when the Japanese Zen master Taisen Deshimaru was asked by his Western students what people should do in their everyday lives, he responded, "Work, go to the toilet, eat; whatever you like." Activist Western Zen teachers have added to Deshimaru's Japanese version of the Zen life, urging their students to be socially active as well. Politically and socially aware, a new generation of Zen Buddhists is paving a contemplative way that blends quite naturally with "turning the Dharma wheel." If the need for such spiritually inspired social action is neglected, the legitimacy of Zen Buddhism in a society that regards ethics and religion as inseparable will eventually be undermined.

The third major trend in Zen practice is the rapid spread of technology across the globe. By the end of the twentieth century, the practice of Zen in many Western centers had become so "radical" that even formal in-person student-teacher interviews had given way to "doku-phone," e-mail, chat room, and "Facebook koan" interactions. As we are daily witnessing the proliferation of newer and faster ways of communicating take hold, we should be prepared for even more radical changes in a global Zen practice that even reformers like Hakuin or Nyogen Senzaki could not imagine.

However, despite these radical changes, Zen has proven flexible in adapting to its new home in the West. Accommodating to democratic decision-making, an inherent distaste for hierarchy, feminist demands, and a deep-seated impulse to do "good works," Zen is changing its monastic robes for clothing that is more appropriate to a communitarian lay society. Inevitably, it will cease to reflect caste structures of the last twenty-five hundred years. Happily, though, it does not seem to be losing its religious function of providing a way toward spiritual freedom.

By its very nature, Zen is contemplative. Zazen means settling oneself away from the world—for half an hour a day, for a weekend, for a seven-day retreat, or for a year. That is the basis for all meditative traditions. The Buddha, a product of his Indian culture, cloistered his students as celibate monks and nuns. As Western laypeople following the Buddha's advice to be our own authorities, we have begun to shape a practice that befits our time and place. But the Zen message remains the same, permitting us to see ourselves everywhere: sometimes as Joshu putting his sandals on his head, or as Unmon shouting, "Sesame rice cake!" sometimes as a fox, and sometimes as an old woman who gets insulted and hits a monk on the head. The magic of Zen lives in the act of sitting; its creativity is expressed in the koan, the manifest world of form inseparable from the wordless, imageless experience of emptiness. It is a place of ceaseless play where we shine with the morning star and fly with the wild goose. Yet it is wedded to the sort of discipline it takes to sit down and meditate seriously for a lifetime while actively engaging in the world as a teacher, a doctor, a mother, a carpenter, even a politician. This is Crazy Cloud Zen. Every child is born to it. Those who grow up to live it with every breath and crook of the finger march alongside Ikkyu through the streets of Sakai on New Year's Day waving a wooden sword as they make their way to work in the morning; sit with Bassui in his cozy tree house as they bake bread; and capture the Unborn with Bankei over an open campfire in a mountain *sesshin*.

Today, even Japan has been jolted into the new lay-driven Zen paradigm, as we witnessed for ourselves on a recent visit to two of Japan's oldest Zen temples. Thinking we were to be taken on a tour, we joined a long queue only to discover that we hadn't joined a group of "tourists" but *sesshin* participants waiting to sign in for a week-long retreat. Having trained with strict monastic Japanese Zen teachers in Japan and the West, we were surprised to find that not only was the leader of the group a woman but that at least half of these lay Zen practitioners were women, outnumbering the resident monks by almost two to one! What surprised us even more was the gentle treatment they were getting: no shouting, no insults, no beatings—all while maintaining the same disciplined silence and "meditative" mode that had been hammered into us by far harsher means over twenty-five years ago. We were delighted to see that the seeds of our own evolving "grassroots Zen" reforms had borne fruit not only in the West but in its ancestral home. How did this happen? Guided by the Zen radicals, rebels, and reformers in this book, we'll try to answer this question by sharing a bit of our own "Crazy Cloud" journey.

We had each spent the early 1980s practicing "samurai Zen" with Japanese Rinzai roshis before heading to Hawaii and becoming lay Zen students of Robert Aitken. Building on this American teacher's peace-oriented practice of Zen with its emphasis on non-violence and social justice, we moved from Hawaii five years later and started the Princeton Area Zen Group. Consciously modeling our practice on "Crazy Cloud" reformist principles, our experience in Princeton among non-resident laypeople, the majority of whom were beginners with no particular interest in monastic Buddhism, convinced us of the need for even more radical changes. Thus, our American "grassroots Zen" practice went even further to accommodate our growing lay community by eliminating remaining monastic trappings such as roshi titles, financial support of teachers, Dharma succession and formal transmission ceremonies, beating sticks, robes, and other priestly regalia. However "radical" this seemed at the time, we still kept to what we felt (and twenty-five years later, still feel) remain essential to a committed Zen practice: daily zazen, retreats, koan practice and interviews, Dharma talks, and chanting of major Zen sutras in Sino-Japanese and English. In the peripatetic tradition of our Crazy Cloud forbears, we again moved on after five years, returning to Princeton to lead sesshin until handing over teaching responsibilities to Bill Boyle in 2005, upon his unanimous confirmation by the PAZG membership. For the past five years we've been dividing our time between Melbourne, Australia, and Honolulu, Hawaii. Our new situation has demanded yet another turn in our practice, one that blends Crazy Cloud and Grassroots Zen with elements inspired by each of our radical forbears.

P'ang Yun and *Ling-chao* continue to serve as models for our family-style, tutorial Zen teaching partnership focused on traditional koan practice with committed individual students outside the zendo.

The marketplace humor and playfully profound koan exchanges of *Rinzai* and *Fukei* provide an indispensible living reminder of the joys of everyday Zen practice.

Bassui's landmark koan "Who is hearing the sound?" brings home the never-ending experience of self-realization associated with the compassionate Bodhisattva Kannon who liberates all beings from suffering.

Ikkyu's rejection of "Dharma transmission" and passionate immersion in "the world of the ten thousand things" simultaneously call our attention to life's changing conditions while precluding any ego-motivated thoughts of empire-building.

Condensing all of Zen in the immediate experience of the moment, *Bankei's* teaching of the "Unborn" points to ordinary life outside the zendo as a fertile field of practice. His independence and secular liberalism are perfectly suited to our American "grassroots" style of free-spirited Zen.

Rejecting the asceticism and self-inflicted pain too often mistaken for Zen "discipline," *Hakuin's* "grandmotherly" concern for his own and his students' physical and mental health are a perpetual reminder that "this very body is the Buddha."

Nyogen's metaphor of Zen as a garden and the Zen teacher as the gardener who never forgets that he or she is "also a flower of the garden" is the core of our egalitarian grassroots Zen practice. No matter where we go, our "floating zendo" with its bells, clappers, sitting cushions, and "Buddha Box" container accompanies us as we follow our "American Hotei" down the Dharma road.

Finally, *Soen's* hearty laughter and thigh-slapping shout of "Just this!" infuse each enlightened step of the journey with spontaneous joy.

While these Zen radicals, rebels, and reformers continue to inspire us, we ought not forget that they were often marginalized, their teachings laundered by traditionalists whose secular connections to the world of power and politics overtook their Crazy Cloud vision of Zen. Ikkyu's voice cries out to call it back, provoking us to leap fearlessly into our creative depths, open to the same wellspring of ebullient energy that fueled his practice, demanding that we scrub the hard stone of the ego down to a pebble, and plumb the darkest depths of ourselves—as artlessly as a kitten tussling a ball of string. P'ang and Nyogen, Rinzai, Hakuin, and Soen have never stopped urging us to stand on our own feet. We just haven't been listening. For too long they have been set outside the mainstream, admired from afar as religious geniuses who were not to be emulated for their "eccentricity," their "anarchism," or, as in Ikkyu's case, their "licentiousness." Crazy Cloud Zen is neither hedonistic nor eccentric. It is the natural development of one whose insight into the ineffable emerges as the most spiritual form of self-expression in *this very body* and in *this very place*. It plays on a formless stage, its spirit expressed in Fuke's cartwheel, Hakuin's caricatures, Ikkyu's comic poetry. It speaks to us in gestures. Like the swaying bamboo or the string bean at the tip of our fork, it invests every moment of our lives with radiance.

Notes on Sources

Introduction
p. 3 "There are neither Buddhas...": Kenneth Ch'en, *Buddhism in China.*

1. P'ang Yun
All direct quotations and poems in this chapter are from Ruth Fuller Sasaki's translation, *A Man of Zen: The Recorded Sayings of Layman P'ang.*

2. Rinzai
All direct quotations in this chapter are from *The Record of Lin-chi,* translated by Ruth Fuller Sasaki, and from Kenneth Ch'en's *Buddhism in China.*

p. 30 "Nowadays, few men...": *Buddhism in China.*

p. 42 "I speak this way...": *The Record of Lin-chi.*

pp. 45–46 "Mind is without form...": *The Record of Lin-chi.*

p. 47 "There are some students...": *The Record of Lin-chi.*

pp. 47–48 "There are some Buddhist...": *The Record of Lin-chi.*

3. Bassui
All direct quotations in this chapter are from Arthur Braverman's unpublished 1989 manuscript, *Bassui Zenji: Talks With Students,* subsequently published as *Mud and Water: A Collection of Talks by the Zen Master Bassui.*

4. Ikkyu

All direct quotations and poems in this chapter are from Sonja Arntzen's *Ikkyu and the Crazy Cloud Anthology* and Jon Covell's *Zen Core: Ikkyu's Freedom.*

p. 79 "From the world of passions…": *Zen Core.*

p. 82 "Robbers never strike…": *Ikkyu and the Crazy Cloud Anthology.*

p. 83 "Greed for luxuries…": *Zen Core.*

p. 86 "After ten days…": *Zen Core.*

pp. 86–87 "I'm a simple man…": *Zen Core.*

p. 88 "I am ashamed…": *Zen Core.*

p. 90 "My hand, how it…": *Ikkyu and the Crazy Cloud Anthology.*

p. 91 "Who carries on the basic…": *Zen Core.*

p. 92 "After my death…": *Zen Core.*

p. 94 "Men in the midst…": *Ikkyu and the Crazy Cloud Anthology.*

5. Bankei

All direct quotations and poems are from Norman Waddell's translation *The Unborn: The Life and Teaching of Zen Master Bankei* and Peter Haskel's *Bankei Zen: Translations from the Record of Bankei.*

p. 104 "I pressed myself…": *The Unborn.*

p. 113 "I've lived for…": *The Unborn.*

pp. 115–16 "You make yourself…": *The Unborn.*

p. 116 "When you're awake…": *The Unborn.*

p. 117 "Try to stay…": *The Unborn.*

pp. 119–20 "Here's something…": *The Unborn.*

p. 121 "My own struggle…": *The Unborn.*

p. 123 "What does it matter…": *Bankei Zen.*

6. Hakuin

All direct quotations are from Philip Yampolsky's *The Zen Master Hakuin* and from Heinrich Dumoulin's *Zen Buddhism: A History*, vol. 2.

pp. 133–34 "Suddenly a great doubt…": *Zen Buddhism: A History*.

p. 140 "In the realm…": *The Zen Master Hakuin*.

p. 141 "I made up my mind…": *The Zen Master Hakuin*.

p. 146 "There are some blind, bald…": *The Zen Master Hakuin*.

pp. 146–47 "Some two hundred years…": *The Zen Master Hakuin*.

p. 147 "The practice of the Lotus Sutra…": *The Zen Master Hakuin*.

pp. 152–53 "A warrior must…": *The Zen Master Hakuin*.

pp. 154–55 "Often Zen masters…": *The Zen Master Hakuin*.

7. Nyogen Senzaki

All direct quotations and poems in this chapter are from Soen Nakagawa et al., *Namu Dai Bosa*; Nyogen Senzaki, *Like a Dream, Like a Fantasy*; Nyogen Senzaki, *On Zen Meditation*; Nyogen Senzaki, *Comments on the Mumon Kan*, unpublished manuscript (published as *Eloquent Silence: Comments on the Mumon Kan*); and Nyogen Senzaki and Ruth Strout McCandless, *The Iron Flute*.

p. 165 "I coined the word…": *On Zen Meditation*.

p. 165 "Brother Nyogen is a…": *The Iron Flute*.

p. 171 "Friends in the Dharma…": *Like a Dream, Like a Fantasy*.

p. 172 "It is not enough…": *Namu Dai Bosa*.

pp. 172–73 "Some Americans pay…": *Comments on the Mumon Kan*.

p. 174 "If anyone makes…": *Comments on the Mumon Kan*.

p. 174 "When my master…": *On Zen Meditation*.

p. 175 "There is no graduation…": *Comments on the Mumon Kan*.

p. 176 "I have no such funny...": *Comments on the Mumon Kan.*

p. 176 "What is this mind...": *Namu Dai Bosa.*

p. 177 "Buddhism counsels...": *Namu Dai Bosa.*

p. 178 "When I was a young...": *Comments on the Mumon Kan.*

p. 179 "It is a pity...": *Comments on the Mumon Kan.*

p. 180 "One hundred thousand Bonzes...": *Comments on the Mumon Kan.*

p. 181 "My ideal life...": *Comments on the Mumon Kan.*

8. Soen

All direct quotations and poems are from *The Soen Roku: The Sayings and Doings of Zen Master Soen*, ed. Eido Shimano, and *Namu Dai Bosa* by Soen Nakagawa et al.

pp. 188–89 "The two of us...": *The Soen Roku.*

p. 189 "My mind ceased...": *The Soen Roku.*

p. 197 "Ordinary is extraordinary...": *The Soen Roku.*

p. 197 "To die is...": *Namu Dai Bosa.*

pp. 198–99 "My friends tell me...": *The Soen Roku.*

p. 199 "Meditation itself is...": *Namu Dai Bosa.*

pp. 199–200 "Cockroach was my pet...": *The Soen Roku.*

p. 200 "All beings are flowers...": *The Soen Roku.*

Epilogue

p. 210 "The uplifted sword...": Robert Aitken, *The Mind of Clover.*

p. 210 "The separation of the absolute...": *The Mind of Clover.*

Glossary

Arhat (Pali) A worthy elder; a Buddhist adept who has not yet gone beyond his or her own enlightenment to save all beings and thus is not yet a bodhisattva.

Bakufu (Jap.) Tokugawa military government.

Bodhisattva (Skt.) Mahayana Buddhist archetype of compassion; one who puts off entering nirvana in a vow to save the many beings.

Buddhadharma (Skt.) Teachings of the Buddha.

Bushido (Jap.) The samurai spirit of the warrior; Japanese militarism; bravery in the face of death.

Chinzo (Jap.) An official Zen portrait of an abbot.

Chonin (Jap.) Townsmen, merchant class of Tokugawa Japan.

Chu-shih (Chin.) Lay Zen practitioners of the T'ang era.

Daimyo (Jap.) A samurai chieftain, head of a clan of retainers.

Furyu (Jap.) Ikkyu's "far out" or "wild" Zen.

Fusho Zen (Jap.) Bankei's form of teaching, with its emphasis on discourse rather than meditation or koans.

Gaijin (Jap.) Foreigner.

Giri (Jap.) Duty.

Goi koans (Jap.) The most difficult form of koan designed to take the student through T'ang master Tozan's "Five Modes of the Apparent and the Real."

Gonsen koans (Jap.) Koans that help to clarify the difficult words and phrases of Zen ancestors.

Gozan (Jap.) "Five Mountain" temple hierarchy created in Japan to emulate a similar arrangement in China, where a few selected monasteries were given special privileges, status, and economic support by the emperors.

Great Death (Jap. *daishi*) A metaphor for *satori*.

Great Doubt (Jap. *daigi*) The "dark night of the soul" preceding *satori*.

Great Joy (Jap. *daikangi*) The flow of love and compassion resulting from the *satori* experience.

Haiku (Jap.) A seventeen-syllable form of Japanese poetry, derived from *renga*, that is associated with Zen themes.

Hara (Jap.) A point for concentration in zazen located two inches below the navel; a center of energy (the site of the vagus nerve).

Hogo (Jap.) Verbal instruction, usually in sermon form.

Hojo (Jap.) Shogun government.

Hosshin koans (Jap.) Intended to deepen the student's insight into his or her essential nature.

Hotei (Jap; Chin. *Pu-tai.*) Chinese folklore character representing Maitreya, the future buddha, who bestows gifts on children.

Inka (Jap.) Seal of enlightenment granted by a Zen master to a disciple in confirmation.

Ji (Jap.) Temple or monastery. For example, Myoshinji.

Jizo (Jap.) A Japanese archetypal "savior bodhisattva" particularly identified with children.

Joriki (Jap.) Concentration power in sitting meditation.

Jukai (Jap.) Ceremony of taking the Buddhist precepts; public declaration of becoming a disciple of Shakyamuni Buddha.

Kami (Jap.) Shinto nature gods. In the Meiji period, the emperor was revered as a living *kami*.

Kannon (Jap.; Chin. *Kuan-yin*) Literally, "The one who perceives the sounds of the world"; the bodhisattva of mercy and compassion.

Karma (Skt.) Buddhist concept of the law of cause and effect.

Kensho (Jap.) Seeing into one's essential nature; another expression for *satori*.

Kessei (Jap.) A two- or three-month training period held twice a year in Zen monasteries.

Kikan koans (Jap.) Lead to a better understanding of the differentiated world of phenomena as seen through the "enlightened eye."

Koan (Jap.) "The relative and the absolute"; Zen meditation technique employing vignettes from ancient exchanges between master and disciple as a focus for concentration; a nonintellectual means for penetrating through dualistic thinking to the Absolute.

Kokushi (Jap.) National Zen teacher; highest honor bestowed on a Zen master by the government.

Koto (Jap.) A Japanese musical instrument resembling a lyre.

Kyosaku (Jap.) The wooden stick used in Zen monasteries to awaken sleepy sitters.

Kyo-un (Jap.) "Crazy Cloud"; the term invented by Ikkyu to characterize his form of Zen.

Mahayana Buddhism (Skt.) "The Great Vehicle"; the Buddhist practice in China, Korea, Tibet, Vietnam, and Japan, with its emphasis on the bodhisattva ideal of saving the beings of the world.

Manjushri (Skt.) The sword-wielding bodhisattva of wisdom who cuts through delusion.

Mentorgarten (Ger.) Nyogen Senzaki's term for his antihierarchical

Zen, where everybody was recognized as both teacher and disciple. Taken from the German educational reformer Froebel's concept of the kindergarten.

Mondo (Jap.) Zen dialogue between teacher and student, or an exchange between Zen adepts expressing the basic truths of the realization experience.

Mukei (Jap.) Ikkyu's pun denoting himself as the "dream boudoir" monk.

Naikan (Jap.) Visual imagery therapy given to Hakuin by Hakuyu the hermit-healer.

Nanto koans (Jap.) Point to the undifferentiated in the midst of daily activity.

Nembutsu (Jap.) "Namu amida butsu"; a mantra reciting the savior Buddha Amida's name over and over again in prayer or meditation; practice instituted by Honen, founder of the Pure Land School of Buddhism in the twelfth century.

Nichiren (Jap.) The Lotus Sutra sect, a popular form of Japanese Buddhism emphasizing devotion and the prayer "Namu myoho renge kyo"—"Hail to the Lotus of the Wondrous Dharma"—which is the first line of the Lotus Sutra. Nichiren, the thirteenth-century founder of this school, proclaimed that the ultimate truth of Buddhism could be found only in The Lotus Sutra.

Ninjo (Jap.) Emotions.

Oibara (Jap.) A samurai's expression of his devotion to his lord by joining him in death.

Paramitas (Skt.) The six "perfections" of Buddhism; for instance, the perfection of wisdom.

Precepts The ethical guidelines of Buddhism, like not killing, not stealing, and so on; the core of Zen ethics.

Renga (Jap.) An open-ended form of Japanese verse improvised in the form of witty repartee in a group.

Rinzai Zen (Jap.) Founded by the Chinese T'ang master Rinzai Gigen (Lin-chi I-hsuan), and introduced to Japan by masters Eisai and Daio in the thirteenth century; emphasizes koan practice.

Roshi (Jap.) "Old teacher"; Zen master.

Saisen-itchi (Jap.) The ancient Japanese concept of the unity of religion and government, revived in the Meiji period.

Sala tree (Skt.) The legendary tree that turned white at the Buddha's death.

Samadhi (Skt.) Absorption in meditation.

Sangha (Skt.) Originally, monastic Buddhist community, extended in the Mahayana tradition to the lay community as well.

Sanzen (Jap.) A Rinzai expression for private interview between Zen teacher and disciple; also called *dokusan* in some traditions.

Satori (Jap.) Self-realization; enlightenment; realization of emptiness.

Seppuku (Jap.) Ritual suicide.

Shi (Jap.) Death; an important koan for samurai training in Zen.

Shiki (Jap.) Japanese civil bureaucracy of the Minamoto period in the thirteenth century.

Shin (Jap.) A particular sect of Pure Land Buddhism, founded by the Buddhist monk Shinran (1173–1262), who promised salvation to all who sincerely called upon the mythical Buddha Amida with the formula, "Namu amida butsu." Shin has been, and continues to be, the most popular Buddhist sect in Japan.

Shingon (Jap.) Literally, "True Word" sect of Buddhism, founded by the Buddhist priest Kukai (774–835). It is derived from Indian and Tibetan Tantrism. Known also as "esoteric Buddhism," it is centered on the belief in the cosmic Buddha

Vairochana, and emphasizes proper ritual performances of mantras (sacred syllables) and mandalas (cosmic icons).

Shinto (Jap.) "The Way of the *Kami* (gods)"; animistic religion centered on ancestor worship and ritual purification; Japanese state religion connected with the figure of the Emperor in the Meiji era.

Shunyata (Skt.) Emptiness; "suchness."

Shuso (Jap.) Head monk.

Soto Zen (Jap.) Derived from the Chinese T'ang masters Tozan Ryokai (Tung-shan Liang-chieh) and Sozan Honjaku (Ts'ao shan Pen-chi), and introduced to Japan by master Eihei Dogen in the thirteenth century; emphasizes *shikantaza*, "just sitting."

Suiboku-ga (Jap.) Japanese ink painting.

Sutra (Skt.) Scripture, discourse, or classic; name given to the sacred texts of the Buddhist canon.

Tathagata (Skt.) Literally, "The one who just comes"; the buddha aspect of potentiality and creation; the immanent form of the Absolute.

Tenzo (Jap.) Monastery cook.

Theravada Buddhism (Pali) "The Way of the Elders"; the "orthodox" stream of Buddhism practiced in Southeast Asia that emphasizes monasticism and enlightenment with nirvana, or extinction, as its goal.

Tripitaka (Pali) Earliest extant records of the teachings of the Buddha.

Unborn Bankei's expression for the Absolute, realized in the everyday.

Unsui (Jap.) Monk; literally, "cloud water," indicating the monk's passing through the world without leaving a trace.

Wabi (Jap.) The Japanese aesthetic ideal of simplicity and starkness.

Zafu (Jap.) Meditation cushions used in zazen.

Zaibatsu (Jap.) Japanese commercial monopolistic elite.

Zazen (Jap.) Sitting meditation.

Bibliography

Aitken, Robert. *Taking the Path of Zen*. San Francisco: North Point Press, 1982.

————. *The Mind of Clover: Essays in Zen Buddhist Ethics*. San Francisco: North Point Press, 1984.

————. *A Zen Wave: Basha's Haiku & Zen*. 3d ed. Tokyo: Weatherhill, 1985.

Arntzen, Sonja, trans. & ed. *Ikkyu and the Crazy Cloud Anthology*. Tokyo: University of Tokyo Press, 1986.

Beasley, W.G. *The Modern History of Japan*. New York: Praeger, 1974.

Bellah, Robert. *Tokugawa Religion*. New York: The Free Press, 1985.

Blyth, R.H. *Zen and Zen Classics*. Vol. 5. Tokyo: Hokuseido Press, 1962.

Braverman, Arthur, trans. *Bassui Zenji: Talks with Students*. Unpublished manuscript, 1989. [Published as *Mud and Water: A Collection of Talks by the Zen Master Bassui*. San Francisco: North Point Press, 1989.]

Ch'en, Kenneth. *Buddhism in China*. Princeton, N.J.: Princeton University Press, 1964.

Chung-yuan, Chang, trans. *Original Teachings of Chan Buddhism*. New York: Grove Press, 1982.

Cleary, Thomas, trans. *Zen Essence: The Science of Freedom*. Boston: Shambhala, 1989.

Cleary, Thomas, and J.C. Cleary, trans. *The Blue Cliff Record.* 3 vols. Boston: Shambhala, 1977.

Covell, Jon, and Sobin Yamada. *Zen's Core: Ikkyu's Freedom.* New Jersey: Hollym International, 1980.

Dumoulin, Heinrich. *Zen Buddhism: A History. Vol. 1: India and China.* New York: Macmillan, 1988.

———. *Zen Buddhism: A History. Vol. 2: Japan.* New York: Macmillan, 1990.

———. *Zen Enlightenment.* New York: Weatherhill, 1983.

Epstein, Perle. *Oriental Mystics and Magicians.* New York: Doubleday, 1975.

Fields, Rick. *How the Swans Came to the Lake.* Boulder, Colo.: Shambhala, 1981.

Fitzgerald, C.P. *A Concise History of East Asia.* New York: Praeger, 1966.

———. *A Short Cultural History of China.* Ed. C. G. Seligman. New York: Appleton-Century, 1938.

Haskel, Peter, trans. *Bankei Zen: Translations from the Record of Bankei.* New York: Grove Press, 1984.

Hoffman, Yoel, trans. *Japanese Death Poems.* Tokyo: Charles E. Tuttle, 1986.

Hoover, Thomas. *Zen Culture.* New York: Random House, 1988.

———. *The Zen Experience.* New York: New American Library, 1980.

Hyers, Conrad. *Zen and the Comic Spirit.* London: Rider, 1974.

Johnson, Wallace. *The T'ang Code.* Princeton, N.J.: Princeton University Press, 1979.

Kapleau, Philip. *The Three Pillars of Zen.* Garden City, N.Y.: Doubleday, Anchor Books, 1980.

Kasulis, T.P. *Zen Action / Zen Person*. Honolulu: University of Hawaii Press, 1981.

Kitagawa, Joseph. *Religion in Japanese History*. New York: Columbia University Press, 1966.

Leggett, Trevor, trans. *A Second Zen Reader*. Tokyo: Charles E. Tuttle, 1988.

Lloyd, Arthur. *The Creed of Half Japan*. London: Smith, Elder, 1911.

McMullen, David. *State and Scholars in T'ang China*. New York: Cambridge University Press, 1988.

Meyer, Milton. *China: An Introduction*. New Jersey: Littlefield Adams, 1978.

Miura, Isshu, and Ruth Fuller Sasaki. *Zen Dust*. New York: Harcourt, Brace, and World, 1966.

Mukoh, Takao, trans. *The Hagakure*. Tokyo: Hokuseido Press, 1980.

Murano, Koken. *Buddha and His Disciples*. Tokyo: Sanyusha, 1932.

Nakagawa, Soen. *The Soen Roku: The Sayings and Doings of Master Soen*. Ed. Eido Shimano. New York: Zen Studies Society Press, 1986.

Nakagawa, Soen, Nyogen Senzaki, and Eido Shimano. *Namu Dai Bosa: A Transmission of Zen Buddhism to America*. Ed. Louis Nordstrom. Bhaisajaguru Series. New York: Theatre Art Books, 1976.

Nakamura, Kichisaburo. *The Formation of Modern Japan*. Honolulu: East/West Center Press, 1962.

Nukariya, Kaiten. *The Religion of the Samurai*. London: Luzac, 1913.

Perry, John Curtis, and Bardwell L. Smith. *Essays on T'ang Society*. Leiden: E.J. Brill, 1976.

Reischauer, Edwin, trans. & ed. *Ennin's Diary: The Record of a Pilgrimage to T'ang in Search of the Law.* New York: Roland Press, 1955.

Sanford, James. *Zen Man Ikkyu.* Chico, Calif.: Scholars Press, 1981.

Sansom, George. *Japan: A Short Cultural History.* New York: Appleton-Century, 1962.

Sasaki, Ruth Fuller, et al., trans. *A Man of Zen: The Recorded Sayings of Layman P'ang.* Tokyo: Weatherhill, 1976.

———. *The Record of Lin-Chi.* Kyoto: Institute for Zen Studies, 1975.

Schloegl, Irmgard, trans. *The Zen Teachings of Rinzai.* Berkeley: Shambhala, 1976.

Senzaki, Nyogen. *Eloquent Silence: Comments on the Mumon Kan,* Ed. Roko Sherry Chayat. Somerville, MA: Wisdom Publications, 2008

———. *Like a Dream, Like a Fantasy: Zen Writings of Nyogen Senzaki.* Ed. Eido Shimano. New York: Japan Publications, 1978.

———. *On Zen Meditation: What a Buddhist Monk in America Said.* Kyoto: Bukkasha, 1936.

Senzaki, Nyogen, and Ruth Strout McCandless. *Buddhism and Zen.* San Francisco: North Point Press, 1987.

———. *The Iron Flute.* Tokyo: Charles E. Tuttle, 1964.

Shibayama, Zenkei. *A Flower Does Not Talk.* Trans. Sumiko Kudo. Tokyo: Charles E. Tuttle, 1970.

Suzuki, D.T. *Essays in Zen Buddhism.* New York: Grove Press, 1984.

———. *Zen and Japanese Buddhism.* Tokyo: Travel Bureau, 1965.

Tanahashi, Kazuaki, trans. *Penetrating Laughter.* Woodstock, N.Y.: Overlook Press, 1984.

Varley, H. Paul. *Japanese Culture.* Honolulu: University of Hawaii Press, 1984.

Waddell, Norman, trans. *The Unborn: The Life and Teaching of Zen Master Bankei*. San Francisco: North Point Press, 1984.

Wright, Arthur. *Buddhism in Chinese History*. Stanford: Stanford University Press, 1959.

Wright, Arthur, and Denis Twitchett. *Perspectives on the T'ang*. New Haven: Yale University Press, 1973.

Yamada, Koun. *The Gateless Gate*. Los Angeles: Center Publications, 1979.

Yampolsky, Philip. *The Zen Master Hakuin*. New York: Columbia University Press, 1971.

Yanagida, S. "The Life of Lin-Chi I Hsuan." *Eastern Buddhist* 5–2 (1972): 70–94.

Index

About the Authors

Recipient of the Theodore Hoepfner Fiction Award and past writer-in-residence at the Mishkenot Sha'ananim Artist Colony in Jerusalem, Pushcart Prize nominee PERLE BESSERMAN was praised by Isaac Bashevis Singer for the "clarity and feeling for mystic lore" of her writing and by *Publishers Weekly* for its "wisdom [that] points to a universal practice of the heart." Her autobiographical novel, *Pilgrimage*, was published by Houghton Mifflin, and her electronic book story collection, *Marriage and Other Travesties of Love*, by Cantarabooks. Her short fiction has appeared in *The Southern Humanities Review, The Nebraska Review, Briarcliff Review, Transatlantic Review, Agni,* and many others. She has written numerous books on spirituality, the most recent of which is *A New Zen for Women*.

Perle holds a doctorate in Comparative Literature from Columbia University. Together with Manfred Steger, she is a founding co-teacher of the Princeton Area Zen Group in Princeton, New Jersey.

A student of Zen for thirty years, MANFRED B. STEGER is the founding teacher of the Princeton Area Zen Group (www.princetonzengroup.org). He and his wife Perle Besserman are deeply dedicated to the cultivation of a Western-style lay practice that maintains the essential elements of Zen—sitting meditation, interviews with a teacher, and silent retreats. A Professor of Global Studies at RMIT University in Melbourne, Australia, Steger has written or edited twenty books on politics, history, and religion, including the bestselling *Globalization: A Very Short Introduction.*

Manfred and Perle divide their time between Melbourne and Honolulu.

Credits

The authors gratefully acknowledge permission to quote from the following works:

A Man of Zen: The Recorded Sayings of Layman P'ang, translated by Ruth Fuller Sasaki et al., copyright © 1976, published by Weatherhill and reprinted by permission.

Ikkyu and the Crazy Cloud Anthology, translated by Sonja Arntzen, copyright © 1986, published by the University of Tokyo Press and reprinted by permission.

The Soen Roku: The Sayings and Doings of Master Soen, edited by Eido Tai Shimano, copyright © 1986, published by the Zen Studies Society Press and reprinted by permission.

The Unborn: The Life and Teaching of Zen Master Bankei, copyright © 1984 by Norman Waddell, published by North Point Press and reprinted by permission.

Zen Core: Ikkyu's Freedom (Unraveling Zen's Red Thread: Ikkyu's Controversial Way), by Jon Carter Covell, published by Hollym International, copyright © 1980 by Jon Carter Covell and reprinted by permission.

The Zen Master Hakuin, translated by Philip Yampolsky, copyright © 1971, published by Columbia University Press and reprinted by permission.

Wisdom Publications

Wisdom Publications, a nonprofit publisher, is dedicated to making available authentic works relating to Buddhism for the benefit of all. We publish books by ancient and modern masters in all traditions of Buddhism, translations of important texts, and original scholarship. Additionally, we offer books that explore East-West themes unfolding as traditional Buddhism encounters our modern culture in all its aspects. Our titles are published with the appreciation of Buddhism as a living philosophy, and with the special commitment to preserve and transmit important works from Buddhism's many traditions.

To learn more about Wisdom, or to browse books online, visit our website at www.wisdompubs.org.

You may request a copy of our catalog online or by writing to this address:

Wisdom Publications
199 Elm Street
Somerville, Massachusetts 02144 USA
Telephone: 617-776-7416 • Fax: 617-776-7841
info@wisdompubs.org • www.wisdompubs.org

The Wisdom Trust

As a nonprofit publisher, Wisdom is dedicated to the publication of Dharma books for the benefit of all sentient beings and dependent upon the kindness and generosity of sponsors in order to do so. If you would like to make a donation to Wisdom, you may do so through our website or our Somerville office. If you would like to help sponsor the publication of a book, please write or email us at the address above.

Thank you.

Wisdom Publications is a nonprofit, charitable 501(c)(3) organization affiliated with the Foundation for the Preservation of the Mahayana Tradition (FPMT).